M000306638

Practical Self-Discipline:

Become a Relentless Goal-Achieving and Temptation-Busting Machine (A Guide for Procrastinators, Slackers, and Couch Potatoes)

By Peter Hollins,
Author and Researcher at
petehollins.com

Table of Contents

Chapter 1. Stop Being So "Lazy"

Lazy. There is so much concealed in such a small word, isn't there?

Have you ever had a day where no matter how hard you tried, you couldn't force yourself to do the tasks you wanted to or were meant to? Maybe you had a day spent wasting time online or watching TV, knowing that assignments, important phone calls, or chores were waiting for you, and yet you just couldn't get any of it done. It may have felt like you were moving in slow motion or just that you had no will to activate your brain from a mode of sloth and sleep. It's a normal feeling, but as with everything, moderation is key.

"*I'm just feeling lazy*" has become a standard way of explaining this inability to find any willpower, passion, or perseverance for a task. But what does it really mean, and does it actually help us understand what's going on in these apathetic moments and help us overcome them?

The trouble with "lazy" is that it doesn't accurately describe the phenomenon we're talking about—and it certainly doesn't offer a clue on how to be better. "Lazy" is a harsh value judgment, and worse than that, it fundamentally misunderstands a particular pattern of behavior. Using "lazy" is lazy, funnily enough.

In the chapters that follow, we'll be looking at this "laziness," not with condemnation but curiosity. What's really happening when we put off tasks? How can we realistically get better—other than self-berating and writing off sluggishness as an unchangeable personality trait? What is the root cause of this inability to do, and how can we train our brains to move past it or at least not make it our default course of action? Why does it feel so damned difficult to lift a single finger sometimes?

But in this first chapter we're going to be taking a different approach entirely. Firstly, we'll dismantle the idea of laziness altogether. *It doesn't exist.* It's an excuse, and as with 99% of excuses, it is a false construction designed to make ourselves feel better (a strong assertion that makes itself obvious only in hindsight, usually).

What does exist, however, are *barriers* to our action. If you look at a person lounging around in front of the TV in the middle of a weekday in their pajamas, while work piles up around them, you might call them lazy. After all, doesn't this schlub have things to do? People are, at the most basic level, actually quite rational creatures, and they behave as they do for a reason. So when a person's behavior doesn't make sense at first glance (i.e., you can't see the reason), it pays to look deeper. To the environmental context. To the barriers. To the invisible obstacles that, once understood, perfectly explain their behavior.

If this is starting to sound more like a psychology book, then the goal is achieved, because any problems we have with self-discipline, self-esteem, self-anything begin with our mindsets and the way we see and observe the world around us. We almost never have external problems; we only have problems of mindset, judgment, and expectation.

Consider procrastination. We all love to heap moral blame, onto ourselves or others, for not doing what we should be doing. The way we talk about procrastination is to condemn it as almost a sin, as a personal weakness. But people are rational and logical actors. So what are we missing? Most of us can see that sinning isn't really the motivation—after all, people procrastinate on tasks they set for themselves, on activities they care deeply about.

So what's going on? If it's not a moral problem, it's an emotional and organizational one. Why do people procrastinate? As far back as 1978, researchers Bem and Funder were showing that *situational constraints* are a far better predictor of behavior than static personality traits. This means that we are more likely to be products of our environments and emotional states, rather than simply having unproductive or lazy personalities.

Barriers, Not Laziness

Let's consider some reasons that people actually procrastinate, act lazy, and turn away from self-discipline. It's time to shine a light into your brain instead of giving you techniques that may or may not work (though we will certainly get to those at the appropriate time).

People procrastinate because they're afraid.

If you associate ending a task with being appraised negatively, or having the result found to be not good enough, it makes perfect sense that you'd avoid ever reaching the end of that task. Some people work extremely hard on a project only to slow right down and hit a block when only 5% of it remains to be done. It's the safe option, really. Others will work themselves into a paralysis—their perfectionism and intolerance for potential failure leaving them unable to even take the first step, lest it's the wrong one. Again, it's safer to remain incomplete than to face a potentially negative judgment, which can have massive detriments to self-esteem.

So right off the bat, we have an explanation for procrastination that's the opposite of common knowledge: in fact, a person may procrastinate *more* if the task is special to them, since more is at stake. You can be motivated, you can have the desire, you can even have financial incentive and a serious time limit—but if your mind has perceived a threat in the task being completed, you can bet it'll do its best to squirm away from that task no matter what.

To support this notion, a 2017 study by Leary et al. showed that self-compassionate people were more likely to take responsibility for their goals than those who self-criticized. This means that the harsher people are on themselves, the more they are going to avoid action and appear to be lazy. Importantly, judgments in the form of calling yourself "lazy" or piling on guilt will only make things worse.

What will make things better and people more likely to act? Anything that relieves anxiety. The paradox is then that "self-discipline" can stem from actively stepping away from a task that's causing you anxiety. Can you reframe things? Can you become aware of exactly what thoughts are causing you to pull back? It might be as simple as giving yourself permission to do things "badly" or to ease off some of the pressure you've put on yourself. Remind yourself that it's okay to feel afraid but that you *can* do it and that you *will* be okay, no matter the outcome of this particular task.

Look closely at your fears. Face them, and speak them out loud or write them in a journal. You may procrastinate writing your book because deep down you're petrified people will think it's bad and won't read it. Sink even deeper into the fear and you may uncover deep feelings of shame or beliefs that you're a "bad" person. This causes anxiety, and anxiety always causes a "fight-or-flight" response—i.e., procrastination and bailing on the plan for your day of productive work.

Instead, understand your fears and know them well. Actually, it's not that difficult to find, and you may not need a therapist to help you get to the root of maladaptive thoughts. You really just need honesty in speaking out loud the feelings and emotions that you want to avoid.

For example, is it really the end of the world if you earn a little criticism for this task? Is it really true that failing once or twice means you're not a good human being worthy of love? Should it really act as a confirmation about some of the worst fears you have about yourself? Perhaps an alternative: isn't it possible to try again, or even worse, can you imagine that your fears are unfounded and that you may even succeed? For some people, facing their fears leads them to an unexpected culprit behind their procrastination—the fear of success!

Fear is often at the root of so much procrastination and avoidance behavior. For some of us, we don't exactly have the thought, "If I complete this task, I'll do poorly and feel bad," but it's more something like, "I can't be 100% certain about how this will turn out, and I'd rather not risk it." Fearing the unknown is present in all of us, to some extent, but it may be more debilitating in those with extreme procrastination problems. It can be the sheer newness and uncertainty of a task at hand that proves frightening and hence becomes something to avoid and put off.

This can happen if we've unconsciously told ourselves that unknown = threatening. Uncertainty can cause anxiety, and rather than court potential catastrophe, a person may choose to put off a potential conclusion instead of facing an unknown outcome. So even if the status quo is quite painful in itself, it's still known and familiar, and clinging to it is preferable to risking something new. This fear can understandably mix with feelings of low confidence and efficacy ("something unpleasant might happen, and I won't be able to handle it"), exhaustion ("I'm too tired to think about something new or different right now"), or fear of success ("If I succeed, everything might change and I don't know if I want that.")

This kind of thinking can take on an obsessive quality, where people make "rules" to mediate some of the anxiety of an overwhelming task. For example, someone might procrastinate going to the doctor because what they discover there might be too much to handle, so they try to reduce uncertainty by "researching" their symptoms extensively so they can feel reassured. If you recognize this in yourself, the first step is to bring these fears out into the light and start facing them, alone or with a therapist. Where you can, try to "rest" these fears and beliefs to gradually start dismantling them.

To illustrate this testing, a woman might find that her procrastination and laziness in speaking up at her workplace comes down to a handful of fears like the above—"I can't be sure people won't judge me harshly"; "If my boss sees me mess up, I'll be fired"; "If I do *too* well they may ask even more of me or criticize me for being too arrogant..."

Realizing that these thoughts are the root of her "laziness," the woman then starts to unpick them by doing a series of "tests" to prove to herself that she's wrong. She might speak up in a meeting, submit smaller tasks when she's feeling unsure and gauging the reaction, or giving herself the chance to notice others in the office who are not fired or chastised simply for being wrong occasionally. Gradually, she reprograms her beliefs and removes the main obstacle to working productively and efficiently.

People procrastinate because they have a fixed mindset.

"I'm not going to try that new task because I've just never been good at similar tasks."

"I don't want to go back to university because I'm too old."

"I've always been this lazy; it's just the way I am."

Carol Dweck's now-famous concept of "fixed" versus "growth" mindsets can tell us a lot about procrastination. A fixed mindset is the belief that intelligence and ability are set at birth and are broadly unchangeable. They're part of the personality, or constitutional. This means there's very little point in trying to change them! A very negative side effect of this belief is the idea that success, if it comes, is natural and that if you're meant to do something well, you ought to do so immediately and with ease. Someone may try a new hobby, find it quite difficult, and throw their hands up and quit, because they believe that they simply weren't born with the requisite intelligence to do it. What's more, they have a low tolerance for being a beginner—they don't want to look like they're unintelligent or make mistakes. So they avoid or procrastinate or fail to take action at all.

The more adaptive and useful mindset is seeing life as a work in progress and the brain as a fluid, trainable thing. This "growth" mindset means that intelligence and ability are developed deliberately, with consistent, slow practice that improves skill in increments. This way, a person is never surprised to make mistakes as they learn—in fact they expect it. They are comfortable with being a beginner, because they understand that mastery is a process. If they begin a task and are not immediately rewarded, they don't quit or procrastinate—they take it in stride and carry on.

If you find yourself with thoughts that hint at a fixed mindset when it comes to the tasks you're avoiding, it may be time to reframe a little. Train yourself to completely forget about the big goal at the end. Focus only on the smaller tasks in the interim. Try to detach your ego from the outcome. Remind yourself that trying and failing is normal and proof that you're learning! It may even help to try focusing on the process instead of the outcome. Plan to do a number of hours, say, rather than assign yourself an impossible and lofty goal at the outset. As a practical example, a poor goal would be "do well on my assignment" whereas a better one could be "try my hardest on my assignment." The latter is less ego- and goal-centered and is more reasonably under your control. Finally, learn to laugh at yourself a little—sometimes "finished is better than perfect"!

Someone might feel that "you can't teach an old dog new tricks" and as a result procrastinates on all those "new tricks." For example, despite being asked repeatedly to go to therapy with his partner, he may refuse, believing that it's just not in his nature to talk about his feelings. Here, as with many cases of procrastination, it can pay to ask sincerely, "What am I really trying to accomplish right now?" and "Why is what I'm trying to do important to me?"

Realizing that, deep down, protecting and maintaining his relationship is worth more than momentarily feeling right, he may have the impetus to push past beliefs that nothing will change or he'll look stupid trying. Reconnecting with this deeper purpose can bring clarity and inspire action. If this rings true for you, ask yourself if momentarily protecting your ego or avoiding the slight embarrassment of failing or being wrong is worth passing up on your dreams and goals. Do you keep a big bank of embarrassing memories of all the times people around you looked a little silly? If not, then don't expect that others will remember your slip-ups either!

People procrastinate because they have low self-confidence.

According to Dr. Lisa Saulsman and the Center for Clinical Interventions, it's natural that people shy away from tasks that might expose any weakness or flaw. If you *think* that you're generally not that great, you might avoid all situations where you have to apply yourself, be appraised or rated, or have your work looked at by others. The belief that we are fundamentally up to the tasks life throws our way is the root of high self-esteem. If this doesn't sound like you, you may have automatically assumed you'll fail and now are procrastinating on the task because you "know" that doing it will expose your weaknesses to others and be painful for you.

If self-belief is low enough, people may stop themselves even from wanting to set goals for themselves, convinced in advance they'd only fail. Unfortunately, this means they never give themselves the opportunity to prove themselves wrong, making this attitude somewhat self-fulfilling. People with severely low confidence will avoid challenging or pushing themselves and cringe away from criticism or failure. What better way to avoid failure entirely than to not even try in the first place?

Someone could start to challenge these limiting beliefs, however, by gently encouraging themselves to take small steps to prove themselves wrong. Sometimes, even deliberately courting a negative outcome can be strangely liberating—a person deathly afraid of sharing their art may suddenly realize they don't actually care so much once they get their first dreaded negative reaction. If you have low self-esteem, it may help to journal down all the ways you've survived and overcome adversity in the past already. Try to find evidence for a new narrative—one in which you are capable and able to deal with what life throws your way.

People procrastinate because the task is confusing or overwhelming.

Often, the barrier is simply that although the alarm bells are blaring in your head—get this done!—you're not at all clear about *how* to do that or what steps to take first. So you turn up to the task filled with the desire and motivation to do good work, but you're confused and have no direction. The thing looks overwhelming. Immediately, your anxiety goes up and your sense of efficacy and confidence goes right down. Though such a problem isn't strictly emotional to start with, it soon leaves you with a bunch of unpleasant feelings that can make you spiral out of control. It's an organizational problem, and this is not something that is ever strictly taught, is it?

Here, the solution is not emotional so much as practical and executive. It's all about carefully dividing tasks up into smaller tasks and completing them in an orderly fashion. Procrastination can happen when there is a lack of organization in the way a task is approached. Sorting through a task step by step can give you a sense of control and order and give you clear, concrete work to do every time you sit down to tackle it. Here, "laziness" tells a very different story about someone's thought process.

A complicated work presentation you need to compile within two weeks can look overwhelming and lead you to procrastinate. Instead of reprimanding yourself for being lazy, though, simply take a deep breath and break the thing down. Ask yourself, "What is the one thing I need to do to start moving again?" Just one thing: what you can do in the next five minutes, for example. Identify separate tasks of researching data, compiling a graph or two, finding images, writing some descriptive text, getting someone to look over the slideshow, adding a list of references or further reading, etc. Don't worry if you don't have a 100% clear picture before you begin. Only aim to make it a little clearer and understand your very next step. Focus on what needs to happen instead of the big picture.

Now, you can relax and let your field of attention shrink down to a more manageable single task, one at a time. Set aside some time and work on just one aspect. Adjust as you go. Feeling confused or overwhelmed is not a cause for alarm— it's simply a little bell inviting you to stop for a moment, reorient yourself to your goals and values, and remember what you were ultimately trying to achieve. What is unnecessary and can be eliminated? What is the core and what is peripheral? Center yourself and wait a moment. Sometimes giving confusion a little *time* is all that's needed to gain some clarity and an idea of what your next step should be.

People procrastinate because they're mentally or physically unwell.

Emotional barriers (like fear of failure or not being good enough) and executive barriers (not knowing how to break an overwhelming task down systematically) are two of the most common reasons for the "laziness" that is procrastination. But there are other barriers too—some of them even invisible to the person themselves. Again, "laziness" takes on a whole different meaning when we can view it through an alternative lens. We might find that we, or others around us, aren't lazy at all.

Untreated anxiety, depression or other mental illness, ADHD, undiagnosed autism, stress, or trauma can hinder the many cognitive processes that need to take place to complete a task. Low confidence and self-esteem can lead to self-sabotage. Physiologically, it's obvious that work is more difficult to stick with if a person is sleep-deprived, undernourished, ill, or uncomfortable. Ask if you're avoiding the task or are just tired, hungry, thirsty, too hot or cold, etc.

On this note, it's worth taking a moment to separate "lazy" from "tired." Sometimes "I don't have the energy" is actually just code for "I have the energy, but I don't want to spend it on this." You may find an overachiever calling their genuine exhaustion "laziness." The socially accepted response to fatigue is to fight against it: drink coffee, push through, and stop whining. But what if we were to force an elite athlete to act in this manner? We would hopefully recognize that rest and recovery are part of the winning equation to be able to push even harder—why should it be any different with our mental energy?

You may find your body forcing you to take a break if you won't heed its polite request for a rest! Here's where self-condemnation and blame enter again and have a disastrous effect. We fear inactivity, rest, or quiet contemplation, and so we browbeat ourselves into doing more when we're tired—or at least making sure we don't actively enjoy our downtime by piling on guilt when we stop!

A little self-awareness and compassion can make the difference. Take a nap and note your feelings toward the task when you're refreshed and rested. Give yourself permission to take a walk and do something else, and see if your motivation returns in time. Be honest about whether you're giving yourself adequate time to sleep and rest. We are not machines, and treating our bodies like they're not allowed to rest can have dire consequences—not to mention making us less productive anyway.

As an example, someone might find they repeatedly have to force themselves through a new project. They stop and ask,

"Is this the most important thing I should be doing right now?" and discover that, in fact, their priority at that moment is not the project but their own rest and well-being. By simply changing your focus from judgment to curiosity, you can start to look at laziness with compassion and empathy and start finding real ways around it. Laziness will seem like a symptom of a bigger problem—one that can always be solved.

Finally, it's worth noting something else that's seldom mentioned: if you're avoiding a task you've told yourself you want to do or should do, take a closer look. You might discover that you *don't* in fact want to do it or that your motivations are external and superficial. In this case your avoidance is really a sign that the task is not something you're truly aligned with. You don't care, you're apathetic, and you would rather clean the bathroom for the fifth time than devote your time to this *thing*. While this isn't always helpful information, don't ignore this warning sign about what you care or are passionate about.

It seems obvious when you say it deliberately: nobody is intrinsically a failure or *wants* to be lazy or weak-willed or apathetic. We don't want to view ourselves that way, and we will engage in mental acrobatics to avoid it. We all have a desire to work meaningfully toward goals that are important to us. If you find yourself feeling lazy, it's almost always a question of removing the barriers and identifying what is actually keeping you from motion. Once the barriers are removed, it then becomes a lot easier to realistically develop self-discipline. It's just about setting yourself up for success rather than continually butting your head against a wall that you cannot identify.

Self-discipline, it's been said, is choosing between what you want *now* and what you want *most*. There is always an opportunity cost, but in truth, the opportunities you are foregoing by acting disciplined aren't very large—comfort, security, safety, television, gaming, junk food, and so on.

Pushing ourselves through our fears, limitations, and bad habits takes energy and is uncomfortable, but is mere discomfort what you will allow to keep you from what you want most?

Takeaways:

- When we label ourselves or others as lazy, are we really doing ourselves justice, or is there more to that simple and overused term? What can we learn about simple laziness to defeat it and perhaps set ourselves up for success?
- Laziness is not so much of a cause as it is a symptom of emotional or organizational issues that are present within our mindsets. It's helpful to view these shortcomings as a series of cause-and-effect actions, because the reasons that we are not acting and not exercising self-discipline are more complex than you might realize. We're not lazy; we have many psychological barriers that keep us firmly rooted in place. Take it easy on yourself, because nothing is as

simple as "I don't want to do it, so I won't!"

- The main causes for so-called laziness include fear of judgment and negative emotion, fixed mindsets that make action feel useless, organizational issues that keep you confused and spiraling, and physical or mental deficiencies such as sleep, rest, nutrition, illness, and lack of alignment. It's not so much that we need to cure these issues, because that is a tall task without dedicated introspection, but if we are more aware of what drives us to act (or not), then we stand a chance of addressing it on a consistent basis. You may never truly overcome all of those issues, but for our purposes, breaking inertia is the goal.

- In the end, whether we are being "lazy" or not, we are putting what we want at the current moment over what we want the most. We are getting distracted by shiny objects and temporary moments of gratification. And yet, what are we prioritizing at the current moment besides comfort and safety? Are those powerful enough motivators for you to

stand between what you want the most?
That's a rhetorical question, by the way.

Chapter 2. Formulas for More

We've spent considerable time acquainting ourselves with the emotional and psychological blocks that could be standing in the way of our action. You may have even started to remove some of these blocks in yourself. Should be easy now, right?

Unfortunately, there are never any shortcuts to anything that is truly worth having. Even once barriers are removed (or, realistically, when we simply become aware and know how they manifest in our daily habits), at some point or another you need to take action, and that inevitably means effort and sometimes outright sacrifice.

There will always be a degree of discomfort involved.

Think of it in terms of a physiological example: you could definitely never succeed at a physically demanding task like training for an Olympic event or losing 200 pounds if you were physically battling an illness or were tired and sick throughout. You could only realistically *begin* once you had removed your physical limitations, but even still, you wouldn't get very far without hard work. That's the discomfort part.

Let's now turn to tools that can help us make this hard work a little more manageable, once the barriers are removed. We'll consider certain formulas that offer us a methodical way of thinking about how to tackle tasks and keep procrastination at bay.

A Flowchart to Action

Dr. Patrick Keelan's flowchart approach is a way to guide yourself to taking the correct action with your task or procrastination issue, using a series of pointed questions.

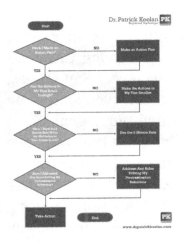

There are four boxes in the flowchart, but you can also think of this protocol as a series of questions—remember, this is a model, so use what practically works for you. The question to answer in the first box is, "Have I made an action plan?" If your answer is no, then, you guessed it, your next step is to make one. This relates to a reason for procrastination we listed in the previous chapter—feeling overwhelmed with a complex task and not quite knowing how or where to start. An action plan means breaking down the task into manageable pieces and setting yourself some goals for completing each one.

It might seem painfully obvious, but deliberately begin by identifying the main aim you wish to achieve. Sometimes, immense clarity can be achieved simply by refining and nailing down your goal. Next, list out separate smaller goals that you have to achieve to reach the main one. Noting how long each will take to accomplish, give yourself a due date for each—remembering again that this is only a *model* and that you are at liberty to adjust accordingly without it being the end of the world!

Remember, too, that even if you've removed the emotional and psychological barriers to you achieving this task, you can still set yourself back by being too perfectionistic, too demanding and judgmental, or too hard on yourself in setting these goals. Shame, guilt, and fear may force a little action from you on occasion, but it will never be the same as working diligently and with passion on a project because you fundamentally want to get it done.

As an example, consider someone who wants to take on the daunting task of selling their car. To help them get it done, they consult the flowchart and ask themselves the first question, "Have I made an action plan?" to which they answer no and proceed to make one. They then list out all the various smaller tasks that need to be done to achieve the larger one—listing the car on some ad sites, speaking to secondhand dealers, chatting to friends to spread the word, deciding on how much to sell it for, checking that its service history is up to date, etc.

Crucially, it's not quite enough to simply list these out—they have to be in some sort of logical order and have to be what you may already know as "SMART" goals. A SMART goal is specific (i.e., not vague), measurable (which means you can quantify it and tell when it's been done), attainable (realistically something you can achieve), relevant (makes sense in the broader context), and time-based (due at some specific point in the future, and not just "someday").

Many people wonder why their daily to-do lists never really help. If you have items such as "sort out tax thing" or "buy healthy groceries," you can understand why this would be the case. What tax thing? How will you know when you can tick this item off the list? And what does "healthy" mean here? How much are you supposed to buy? So a goal like "find out precisely when tax return due date is by the end of today" is a smarter goal.

This leads to the next part of Keelan's flowchart: the question "Are the actions in my action plan small enough?" Maybe you're guilty of having a to-do list that goes, "Buy cat food, email report, fix life." It's clear: tasks that are too big simply don't get done. They overwhelm and lead to procrastination. So double-check that the items you've listed are well and truly single actions, not many actions disguised as a single one. You need to schedule a specific action at a specific time. For example, tomorrow morning you will call a therapist and book an appointment. Then, the following morning, you'll jot down some notes on what you want to discuss in your first session. The next week you'll go to your first session, and so on.

One of the great things about setting up lots of smaller tasks for yourself is the sense of achievement and feeling "unstuck" that comes with completing the task one small piece at a time. Be conscious of this effect and acknowledge and praise yourself for completing small steps. Really appreciate that each task brings you closer and closer—this is essentially the emotional antidote to the stress and avoidance of procrastination.

Again, you have to actually tackle each task, but the beauty is now that, when they're so small, you'll find them far easier to manage and complete. Onto the next step of the flowchart: asking the question "Have I used the five-minute rule when my motivation to take action is low?"

Let's look a little closer at what the five-minute rule is. Simply, you only have to commit to taking action for five minutes. Again, you trick yourself into getting started by lowering the stakes and committing only to getting started. Just force yourself to do the task for five minutes. If you're feeling sluggish, you may even find yourself setting a timer. A little magic happens, however, once you've gotten over the initial hurdle and into the momentum of actually doing the task—i.e., you may notice that you're okay with continuing and press on. This is a great feeling.

Even if you do choose to stop after five minutes, celebrate that it's five minutes more than you otherwise would have done and try again later. The nagging sense of inertia that comes with procrastination can be so paralyzing at times—this rule gets you active again, even if only for a moment, and gives you a little motivational boost.

Another trick that some people find helpful is to quickly dispatch any tasks that only take a few seconds or a minute to do. While you want your tasks to be small, many that float into our daily lives would be better done immediately, without taking the time to dawdle and deliberate over them. If you receive an email that will only take 15 seconds to reply to, just do it, there and then. You might feel some relief at shaving down an enormous task by doing the really obvious, quick tasks right off the bat. This can sometimes be enough to have your motivation kick in.

As an example, someone who has to do a very boring task of sorting through a storeroom may have no real emotional blocks to doing so—it's just a boring task they'd rather not do. They could commit to at least tackling a small corner of the room and set a timer. At the five-minute mark they're in the middle of it and finding the clearing up rather satisfying, and so they push on for another 10 minutes before stopping. All in all, 15 minutes were done on a task that may have easily been put off until tomorrow.

Now, the last box. Ask yourself, "Have I addressed any rules driving my procrastination behavior?" Here, Keelan's "rules" are assumptions, thoughts, or beliefs underlying our procrastination. Like many psychologists, he suggests that our rules will take the form of perceived gains we expect to achieve by procrastinating. This is a slightly different way of thinking about what we've already addressed in a previous chapter. We can think of the barriers to action in another way—as relative benefits of staying inactive.

For example, the barrier we considered earlier (i.e., the fear of being seen and criticized) can be reworked as a benefit (staying safe and uncriticized) or an unconscious rule ("if I play small and don't put myself out there, then nobody will ever criticize me and I won't have to feel bad").

As in the previous chapter, the assumption is that "laziness" is there for a reason and serves a purpose. Find out why you procrastinate, then remove that reason/impediment. We've already covered many of the flavors of human avoidance and the "rules" we set up to protect us but which ultimately don't serve us. However, your reasons for procrastinating are going to be uniquely your own, and only an honest appraisal of your own habits will reveal anything useful.

It may take time to unravel the mess of bad habits, low self-confidence, self-fulfilling prophesy, fear, genuine laziness, unfamiliarity, and plain-old being unskilled to get to the bottom of your procrastination problem—but it's worth it. Be honest with yourself. Be gentle—you're not going on an inquisition to catch yourself out—but be realistic too. A person may, as an example, find that behind their "laziness" is a handful of rules such as "If I don't perform well, people won't expect much of me in the future and I'll be relieved" or "I don't actually want to do this task but I'm unwilling to take the leap and not do it, so I'll make excuses or avoid it for as long as possible" or "If I procrastinate and it inconveniences people, they may just end up doing it for me, which would be really convenient."

In such a case, not only will this kind of honest examination shed light on why the procrastination is happening, but it may help you on a deeper level. You may be able to finally face an uncomfortable truth—that you need to make some changes in life and are not happy with the direction your career or relationship is taking, for instance. Here, pushing through procrastination and doing tasks you ultimately don't want to do wouldn't help—only considering the deeper reasons behind it would. Again, go in with curiosity and not with judgment. This flowchart places these psychological and emotional hurdles at the end, whereas you could also address them first—what matters is that you do address them, one way or another.

A final thing to bear in mind with models or formulas like this one is that, if you're clever, you can inadvertently use the method to procrastinate further. Don't fall into the trap of analysis paralysis or continuing to seek further information or organization before you act. This can waste time and be a convenient way to avoid taking action. After all, what better excuse is there for not doing your work than *preparing* to do your work? So again, it pays to remember that at some point, there's no getting around the fact that if you want to achieve a goal, you need to act. Consistently.

A Formula of Flow

If you use them appropriately, though, formulas can be very useful. Another possible formula to consider is *flow theory*, originally introduced in the '90s by psychologist Mihaly Csíkszentmihályi with his best-selling book, it may appeal to those who find flowcharts and checklists a little too robotic and joyless. Since its inception, the theory has spawned countless research papers and studies confirming its value in improving sports performance, gaming, creativity, and even martial arts.

This model takes into account the nature of both the task at hand and you, the person doing the task. The state of flow is described as one in which, rather than forcing yourself to soldier on in an activity that is mildly unpleasant but has to be done (kind of like eating a vegetable you hate), you do your work with a feeling of joy and ease, completely losing track of time. Most of us have in fact already experienced this flow state already, whether we were aware of it or not.

In flow, you are completely absorbed in the task in front of you, and your attention is not divided. What "flows" is the work itself, moving seamlessly, almost as though it was carrying itself along. People who experience flow while making art or engaging with a passion can find it feels almost spiritual at times, and a complete dissolving of self leads to nothing but the task coming to the fore. Crucially, in a state of flow, a *lot* of stuff gets done.

So how can you induce this state in yourself? The theory says that our experience of doing a task rests on two fundamental features: the "challenge level" of the task and the "perceived skill level." These can each be high, low, or moderate and combine in various ways to produce states like boredom, worry, relaxation, and, if conditions are just right, flow. This concept can be visualized as a graph with two axes—challenge and skill—and the result of their possible combinations.

Let's consider some examples. A task that is not at all challenging but is done by someone who perceives their skills to do that task as low is likely to lead to the emotional state of apathy. The higher that person's perceived skill, however, the more the feeling shifts to boredom, then to relaxation at a very high level of perceived skill. This means that the same task of, say, sewing on buttons to clothes may leave some people feeling completely apathetic, while others will find the task easy and relaxing.

If the challenge level on the other hand is very high, but the perceived skill level is low, then you're bound to feel some anxiety—makes sense if you continually feel unable to rise to the demands of the task! Increase your perceived skill and that anxiety calms down to mere arousal, which, with even more skill, eventually turns into that coveted state of flow. Flow is therefore a state where both the challenge level of a task and your perceived skill at doing it are high.

This is important. It means that tasks are not intrinsically satisfying or difficult or boring and so on. Rather, it is our unique relationship to them and how we rate their difficulty and our own skill in working with them that matters. Interestingly, easy tasks do not lead to flow—we need to be moderately or substantially challenged to enter this state. Likewise, there is seldom a sense of flow felt when we do work that doesn't require skill—a sobering thought.

Wrapped up here in this theory are seemingly both the emotional and cognitive elements we've considered in previous sections. Work that is challenging enough but not too challenging doesn't cause us to feel unconfident, and the fear barriers we've explored may well come down to our lack of *perceived* skill or the task simply being too hard or inappropriate for us.

If you want to reach that inspiring state of mastery, where even complex and difficult tasks seem effortless and joyful, you'll need to continually be aware of how these two factors—challenge and skill—are interplaying. Seek a balance so that you are always where you need to be.

For Csíkszentmihályi, there are three key components that must be present if we hope to achieve the flow state. The first is *goals*. That we need goals to motivate and inspire us is no surprise. The flow should ideally be *toward* something—we are building a complex puzzle, composing music, untangling a challenging problem, or mastering a dynamic set of movements, all toward some clearly conceived end.

We've already seen how important it is that goals are SMART goals and that you're taking the time to break them down into manageable chunks. As an example, you might find it helpful to have a mission statement hung above your home office desk or an inspiring photo or quote that reminds you of what you are ultimately trying to achieve. You may have a vision of your end goal that is encapsulated in a symbol or phrase that you pause occasionally to remind yourself of.

The second required component is *balance*. This is the part where you find a perfect blend of challenge and skill level—having one drastically outweigh the other isn't likely to create flow. Remember, however, that it's *perceived* flow, and it only comes down to you. If a task that everyone thinks is easy feels difficult to you, then it's a difficult task, period. Likewise, don't go on other people's appraisals of your skills—go on your own (all the more reason to make sure you're not working with a low self-esteem).

Finally, the third component is *feedback*. People need to have direct and honest feedback immediately so they can adjust and improve. It's easy to see why—nobody wants to labor away with no idea of whether they're on the right track, if they're improving or getting worse, or indeed if their efforts are appreciated or making any noticeable difference.

Granted, many goals are not something you can realistically expect to get feedback from others for. In this case, "feedback" means your own deliberate awareness of your progress and your own ability to appraise yourself and ask both what you're doing right and what needs to improve. Keep track of your progress (perhaps alongside your goals you've put on the wall) and regularly pause to appreciate how far you've come. Be honest about how you could be better, and actively ask, "What am I not seeing here?" Similarly, feel pride and accomplishment when you do well— internalize that sense of competency. This gives you the opportunity to rebalance your challenge versus skill as your skills improve.

Setting goals, balancing challenge to your current skill set, and regularly checking in to receive feedback will go a long way to cultivating that supremely enjoyable and productive state called flow. In this state, you can achieve more... and enjoy the process. Granted, you're not going to experience joy and ease in every task you have to do throughout the day, and it's unrealistic to expect it. But if you're experiencing procrastination often, look at the problem through this lens and ask whether the challenge and skill levels respectively are too high or low. Remind yourself that there is no universal way that we respond to tasks—we are all individuals with individual limits and strengths. Ask how you are managing with a task and adjust it as necessary.

Be aware, however, that this model doesn't account for being *too challenged*. In the graph, the challenge level rises indefinitely, but in the real world, there are likely to be hard limits. Keep a realistic definition of "challenging." You should be able to actually attain and achieve your goals, without feeling stressed, overwhelmed, anxious, or bad about yourself. Challenge doesn't mean repeatedly subjecting yourself to the experience of failure or doing things at breakneck speed. This will only lead to anxiety. So keep in mind that you may actively need to decrease the challenge level of a task to feel more productive— permanently or at least until your skills can match it.

As an example, consider a young athlete training for his sport. His coach understands that he needs consistent, appropriate challenge to develop his skills and strengthen his body. Daily drills and exercises could be followed, but when the coach notices that the athlete is beginning to panic often, feeling nervous or stressed, he takes it as a sign that either the challenge is too high or the skill is too low. He eases off the pressure and works on developing the athlete's confidence again with more drills. Similarly, when he notices the athlete getting bored or breezing through exercises, he ups the challenge a little. He notices that when the balance is right, and he is consistently giving feedback on how well the athlete is meeting his goals, the state of flow comes easily, and training becomes productive and enjoyable.

An Equation for Doing

Yes, you read that right—someone has formulated an equation of procrastination, one that elegantly works out the interaction of variables that make procrastination more likely to occur.

That someone is Piers Steel, a leading researcher on procrastination. Steel distilled and synthesized 691 studies on the subject to come up with a comprehensive, evidence-based equation that explains motivation and procrastination.

It is known as the "procrastination equation," and Steel drew up the formula as follows:

$$Motivation = \frac{Expectancy \times Value}{Impulsiveness \times Delay}$$

In the equation, motivation pertains to your drive to do your intended task. The higher your motivation, the less likely you're going to procrastinate. The lower your motivation, the more likely you're going to procrastinate.

As shown in the equation, your level of motivation depends on four variables: (1) expectancy, (2) value, (3) impulsiveness, and (4) delay.

Expectancy refers to your expectation of succeeding at the task. For example, if you need to deliver a sales presentation, expectancy pertains to how much you expect the presentation to be a success, as evidenced by your client buying your product or simply by your effective delivery of the presentation. Note that the expectancy variable is in the numerator of the equation. This means that the higher your expectancy of success, the more motivated you're going to be to work on your task.

Value pertains to the importance, worth, or pleasantness of the task. How much does your intended task matter to you? How much do you like doing that task? Your answers to these questions speak of the value you attach to the task. If the sales presentation you're about to do matters very much to you, and/or you actually like working on a sales presentation, then you're more likely to be motivated to get going on it.

Like the expectancy variable, the value variable is also in the numerator of the equation, which means the more you value the task, the greater your motivation for doing it is.

Now let's talk about the two variables in the denominator of the equation: impulsiveness and delay.

Impulsiveness refers to your tendency to act on your impulses immediately, without first thinking through their consequences. The more impulsive you are, the more likely you tend to follow your desires and urges at the drop of a hat. From this description, you can imagine just how being impulsive is related to procrastinating.

For example, let's say that in the middle of preparing for your sales presentation, you feel the urge to check on your social media accounts. If you have an impulsive personality, you'll feel strongly compelled to act on that urge, thus lowering your motivation to focus on the task and leading you to procrastinate instead. This is the reason why impulsiveness is in the denominator of the procrastination equation. Its relationship with motivation is inverse: the more impulsive you are, the less motivated you'll be to work on your intended task.

Finally, there's the variable called delay.

Delay pertains to the interval of time between your completion of a task and your receipt of the reward for doing so. For instance, suppose you've been told that the cash incentive for successfully delivering your sales presentation wouldn't be given to you until your retirement. How would you feel about working on that presentation now?

Such a long delay between your task completion and its reward is likely to decrease your motivation for working on it. The longer you expect to wait for the payoff, the more difficult it is for you to push yourself to get going on the task. This is why the delay variable is in the denominator of the equation. Like impulsiveness, its relationship with motivation is inverse: the greater the delay of the reward, the lesser motivation you'll feel to work on the task.

In summary, here is what's at work when it comes to procrastination: the more you expect to succeed and the more you value a task, the more you're motivated to work on it, and therefore, the less likely you're going to procrastinate. On the other hand, the more impulsive you are and the more delayed the payoff for the task is, the less you're motivated to work, and therefore, the more likely it is that you're going to procrastinate.

And now to answer the million-dollar question: how do you manipulate those variables to beat procrastination?

The beauty of arranging the components of procrastination as variables in a mathematical equation is that you get to clearly see which components you need to increase and which you need to decrease. Let's take a look at the general equation again:

$$Motivation = \frac{Expectancy \times Value}{Impulsiveness \times Delay}$$

Given the equation, the formula for increasing motivation—and therefore decreasing procrastination—is simple: increase the numerators (expectancy and value) and decrease the denominators (impulsiveness and delay).

You may choose to implement a combination of those techniques to increase your motivation, depending on what best applies to your situation.

For example, if you already have high expectations of success and attach a high value to the task but tend to be highly impulsive and easily give in to temptations, then you know you've got to work on decreasing the impulsiveness variable—so maybe try to eliminate distractions in your environment and practice being more thoughtful rather than being overly reactive.

If you aren't impulsive but tend to procrastinate because you lack self-confidence and expect failure, then work on increasing your expectancy for success by working to discover your strengths and learning how to apply them to succeed in your task.

Let's consider how manipulating the procrastination equation would look when applied to our earlier scenario of being tasked to deliver a sales presentation. Remember that given the variables in the procrastination equation—expectancy, value, impulsiveness, and delay—there are at least four ways you can go about increasing your motivation to work on this task.

First, increase your expectancy of success. Put simply, you need to be more optimistic. Think positive! Concrete strategies to help you do so include watching motivational videos, calling to mind situations in the past in which you've succeeded, and engaging in visualization.

Believe in your capacity to do the presentation well and visualize a scene in which your audience is interested and captivated by your presentation and your client reacts positively to your pitch. To prevent this visualization from being just a daydream, though, researchers suggest employing a technique called mental contrasting.

After imagining your presentation going well, mentally contrast that with the actual situation you're in right now. How much work have you really done at this point to be able to realize that vision? This technique is effective at jumpstarting planning and action, driving you to move yourself from your current situation to a successful outcome.

Second, increase the value of the task to you. If doing a sales presentation is something you already highly value because you find it worthwhile or enjoyable, then you don't need to do much more other than continually remind yourself of why it's valuable to you. But if doing the presentation is something you dislike or find meaningless, then your task is to find an aspect of it you could like or to create meaning in the task.

The art of self-motivation has a lot to do with managing your own perceptions. To increase task value, you may consider how doing that sales presentation well could have repercussions on your career progression and, ultimately, your quality of life. Reframe the task not as an end in itself but as a means to an end you value, and you'll find yourself better motivated to get going on it.

Third, decrease your level of impulsiveness. While some people tend to be inherently more impulsive than others, everyone can implement strategies to decrease their overall impulsiveness.

These strategies will need you to modify and structure your environment in such a way that you'll have fewer opportunities to act on your impulses. Suggested by Steel, this approach needs you to "throw away the key." For instance, while working on your sales presentation, close all other tabs on your computer that may tempt you to procrastinate (e.g., YouTube, Facebook, Instagram pages). Don't work in front of the TV.

Eat a good meal before sitting down to work so that you won't be tempted to get up for snack time again while you're working.

Finally, decrease the delay of the reward after task completion. While this variable is less likely to be in your control than the other components (e.g., you're usually not the one who has a say on when you're going to get compensated), there are still ways you can tweak this variable to your advantage. For instance, break down the task into smaller subtasks and reward yourself for completing each of those subtasks.

That way, you can keep feeding your motivation with little reinforcements throughout the process of working on that larger task. Think of it as continuing to feed the fire with small sticks in order to keep it burning. In making your presentation, for instance, reward yourself with a nice meal or a movie when you complete a subtask, such as completing the presentation outline.

By knowing how to steer each of the equation variables in just the right direction, you'll have the power to increase your motivation level and decrease your procrastination habits as you please.

Takeaways:

- We've gone through some of the psychological beasts that underlie the feeling of "lazy" and it turns out that we are beset by barriers, rather than a preference to be sloths. So what can we do with this knowledge? It doesn't automatically launch us into action, but this chapter is about the second-best thing—providing formulas and workflows of sorts to break down what is missing from action. This way we don't have to feel like we are winging it and instead can follow a set of simple instructions to get things done and exercise self-discipline.

- The first set of instructions comes in the form of Patrick Keelan's flowchart for action. He accurately sees that much of laziness comes from a lack of planning and presence, and his flowchart for action contains four simple steps to move you from Point A to Point B. Action plan? Are the steps small enough to act upon? Have I used the five-minute rule? Do I have any beliefs or rules keeping me back? Within each of those steps is also the solution to move to the next step of action.

- The second set of instructions comes from Hungarian writer Mihaly Csíkszentmihályi and his flow theory. Flow is about moving and working effortlessly, to the point that you lose track of time and are engrossed in your task. Sounds nice, doesn't it? He lists a set of requirements for achieving flow, but we will focus on the elements of having your actions pointed toward specific goals, a balance of challenge and ease, and feedback to let you know that you are making a difference, thus keeping you motivated toward chasing that feeling.

- Finally, we come to a set of instructions from Piers Steel, dubbed the procrastination equation. He states that motivation = (expectancy + value) / (impulsiveness + delay). First of all, are you even considering each of these four factors when it comes to trying to take action? Are you aware of what's involved? Next, manipulate these motivating factors into a quantity or order that makes the most sense for you. You'll quickly find what helps your sense of self-discipline, a term that, like "laziness," has several layers to it.

Chapter 3. The All-Powerful Schedule

So far, we've spoken briefly about making lists, breaking tasks into chunks, and then scheduling to do them at various times. Let's now take a more detailed look at what this actually entails—proper schedule technique isn't necessarily common knowledge! Before we begin, however, it should be noted that although there are many different techniques and approaches (some of them directly contradictory, as you'll soon see), there isn't a "right" way, except for the way that practically works for you and gives you the results you want.

First, consider a basic fact: time is limited, and time is in fact all we have when it comes to completing tasks. A calendar is just a piece of paper (or digital equivalent), but it represents the available time you have to devote to achieving your goals. The technique of "timeboxing" is something that will seem obvious and natural to some but a complete revelation to others.

Timeboxing

The principle is simple. Your to-do list only really comes alive when you take the time to convert each task into a "box" of time on your schedule or calendar. To timebox, you allocate a fixed period of time to work on a certain task. That's it. Though simple, it means you'll be more focused, more efficient, and more consciously balanced in how you tackle the smaller tasks we've already discussed creating.

It's a straightforward technique but needs to be done right. First, consider the tasks or area of life that you'd like to try timeboxing. You can apply this to work, your social life, a fixed project, or all your projects in general—it's up to you. Let's say that you're a person from one of the previous examples, and you worked carefully on your emotional barriers causing you to procrastinate, but you still needed a way to realistically plan out your task. You might sit down and timebox for an important work presentation after breaking it down into smaller chunks that then go in your schedule.

A big consideration is the length of the timebox. You can make this what you like, although the hours in the day naturally break down into 15-, 30-, or 45-minute chunks. Less than 15 minutes and you risk skimming the surface and not doing any real work, and more than 45 minutes and you may start fatiguing, getting distracted, and generally earning diminishing returns as your attention and energy flag. Just as you need to rest between reps and sets when you physically train, your brain also needs to take pauses and recoup before it can carry on with a task.

Consider the length of your breaks. Bear in mind what we now know about the state of flow and how perfectly balancing perceived skill with perceived task challenge can allow us to work easily for long periods without even noticing. There are no easy rules for how long your work and break periods should be. These are going to be unique to you and will vary with the task at hand, the day, or even the time of day. As usual, pay attention and notice how you feel, whether you're procrastinating, and how productive you really are.

If you feel like you could do more at the end of a 30-minute chunk, make a note and extend it for next time. If a five-minute break isn't doing the trick, extend it and see what happens. It's important to try to make the contrast between break and work clear: physically step away from the activity, stretch and take a deep breath, go outside, do something different. It's not really a break if your brain is still whirring along with the task or if you just switch browser tabs online and waste time for a few minutes!

If the task is a new, extra-challenging one or something that you know pushes your emotional buttons somehow, you might need a smaller box and a longer break. Don't be afraid to take breaks—the person who takes them wisely is always more productive than the person who forces themselves through fatigue only to find themselves procrastinating for a whole week later because they're burnt out.

As you go through your to-do list and put boxes of time in your calendar according to the task and the length of your work period and rest periods in between, you also want to think of the bigger picture. We're not robots, and throughout the day we all have peaks and troughs of energy and periods where we're naturally more productive. Simply observing your ebb and flow of energy over two weeks or so will show you when your most productive peak is. Most people find that 11:00 a.m. or so is their most productive time.

It makes sense to schedule your most challenging, most important, or most urgent tasks for when you're most productive. Similarly, give yourself a break when you're naturally lower-energy. For your downtime, schedule activities that are less demanding or less important, like housework, planning the next day, or meal prep (assuming these are in fact less demanding from your point of view). Also keep in mind that you will need rest periods, and for those workaholics among us, scheduling nonnegotiable relaxation time is key to honoring the need for rest and taking some time for self-care.

This leads to the next (optional) consideration for learning to timebox effectively, and it's whether to go with "hard" or "soft" timeboxes. Let's say you set a timer and after 45 minutes the timer goes off, but you're right in mid-flow, busy with an activity you don't want to drop. What then? Also, what if you're a few minutes away from the timer ringing but you *really* can't push yourself to do any more?

A hard timebox is one in which you stop and start on the clock according to your plan, no excuses, whereas a soft one can be negotiated either way somewhat. Remember, timeboxing is not about bullying yourself and it's also not about giving yourself endless room to slack off. As we discussed, you'll need a period of adjustment as you observe and learn what works for you. You might start with all soft timeboxes until you know what works.

It's a great idea to assign hard boxes to those tasks you know are a little challenging or you know you'll be tempted to procrastinate with. Use soft boxes for those tasks that are less defined or less urgent or else a task you're unsure of for the moment. On the other hand, some people find hard boxes helpful if they're the type of people who push too hard, overwork, or are "perfectionists," whereas soft boxes are better for those who are trying to catch their "flow" whenever they can.

As an example, imagine a couple are planning their wedding. They know that as the date approaches they have to get organized, but procrastination is creeping in. They realize that the rubber eventually has to hit the road—the wedding is important, so they commit to doing something to make the planning easier. There's lots to do, so they sit down and identify their main goal—completely organizing their dream wedding by a certain date—and use timeboxing to do it. They decide on one 30-minute box every evening when they know they'll be together but after their more pressing day jobs are finished.

They break down the project into several smaller tasks, then divide them up according to their mutual abilities (e.g., the one who finds a particular task less challenging gets to do it). They make the timeboxes soft since they've never planned a wedding before and don't really know how long they'll need, but they agree to adjust as they go. Every evening, they plan the following night's tasks and reevaluate, ordering flowers, ironing out catering details, buying shoes, etc. With a blend of focus and flexibility, they are able to get the job done efficiently with minimal drama and time spent.

With timeboxing, the principles are simple but getting the attitude just right is vital. The point is never to make yourself a slave to your calendar or force yourself to go through tasks with robotic mindlessness. Remember that it's only a technique that is meant to serve you and the goals you care about. You're the only one who is ultimately accountable for how (and whether!) you work, and you get to make the call on whether something is helpful or not. The final thing to remember about timeboxing is that it's meant to be flexible, and you're meant to adjust it as you go. Stop and evaluate frequently to make sure you're actually being more productive (without making yourself miserable).

Don't be afraid to make adjustments or experiment with something completely new. It's okay to realize that, with limited time, you might have to drop the nonessential boxes completely. Try both digital and old-fashioned paper methods.

Closely watch your energy levels, not just the clock. If you stumble on a schedule you like, why not use it for the whole week? And if you earnestly try this approach for weeks and find that it does nothing for you, relax and know that you have full permission to drop it and try something else entirely.

One thing you might notice as you get more familiar with this technique is where your time and attention are *actually* going throughout the day. Are you suddenly alarmed to see just how hard it is to focus for a solid 30 minutes? Keep track of how often you're distracted by your phone or something online and you'll get a real insight into just how much of your time is leaking away instead of being channeled to your goals. If you timebox, at some point or another you're going to have to develop a plan for dealing with distraction and managing the oceans of superfluous information that comes our way every minute.

If all this talk of timeboxing and to-do lists and schedules has left you cold, you're not alone. If you've battled procrastination before, you might have read the previous section with a vague sense of distrust or amusement, having tried these methods yourself and maybe noticed that they even tend to *worsen* procrastination. Again, though, what works for some might not work for others.

Unscheduling

Enter *unscheduling*. Devised by author of *The Now Habit*, Neil Fiore, this approach is designed to tackle procrastination from the completely opposite direction as timeboxing does. This approach is excellent for those struggling to make normal scheduling techniques work for them or those who feel overburdened by guilt when they do procrastinate. The mind is a tricky thing. Waking up each morning to stare down a demanding to-do list can be the very thing that provokes guilt, resistance, and the deep feeling that life is simply a joyless conveyer belt.

Instead, unscheduling starts on the other end, far from the task and stated goal. First schedule all those things you can't help but do—eat, sleep, commute, groom. Next, schedule in those things you need to do to maintain your mental and physical well-being, like running, the gym, meditation, or therapy. Next, schedule in necessary playtime and relaxation, like time for hobbies or being with friends and family. According to Fiore, a minimum of one hour a day and a day a week of leisure time is needed.

Sounds good, doesn't it? Even better, you don't schedule actual work. You only record work done once you've spent at least 30 minutes doing it. The idea is to shift your focus: your life is rich and filled with varied activities, one of which is work, loosely interspersed with all the rest—it's not a wall-to-wall list of overwhelming expectations, leaving your human needs as an afterthought.

What's great is that this approach really seems to work for some people, despite being literally the opposite of what most productivity gurus recommend. Its power lies in how swiftly it removes the heavy emotional burden of setting your life to revolve around a series of tasks. You cut down on self-criticism, guilt, boredom, and the feeling of forcing yourself. The magic is that with this approach, you could end up actually *wanting* to do work you might ordinarily have avoided like the plague.

As with the timeboxing technique, there are a few things to keep in mind if you're to practice unscheduling effectively. Begin with those hours in your day that are spoken for—sleep, commuting, health activities, classes, cooking, etc. Add in leisure time, and don't skimp. It might feel weird at first to tell yourself "you *must* play and relax," but essentially, you must.

Two realizations come from this first step. The first is that you don't have nearly as much time as you thought you did. Many of us assume that we have "24 hours a day" when in fact the amount of time we have to work, after sleep and everything else, is far,

far less. It's unavoidable: if you want to get something done, you'd better do it—you don't have endless time.

The second realization is that you are not a lazy good-for-nothing if you get to the end of the day not having accomplished everything on your mountain of a to-do list. With unscheduling, you have a record of where all your time *did* go. It went to other important, unavoidable things. To maintaining your health and relationships. To cleaning and traveling and sleeping and enjoying yourself. In other words, to being alive! This shift can be incredibly freeing. You are so much more than a machine whose worth rests solely on your output within a very narrow range of activities (i.e., economic ones). If you're the kind of person who beats yourself up at the end of every day because you've "done nothing," this reframing can be surprisingly empowering.

If you succeed with unscheduling, you may find yourself heaving a sigh of relief as untold burdens are lifted off you, and for the first time you may actually feel what it's like to start working on a project because you *want* to. Without trying, you may become more productive anyway. A little paradoxical Zen in your daily work schedule. So instead of starting each morning and looking at your day like it's a boring, burdensome inbox and nothing more, prioritize your well-being, joy, and sense of personal satisfaction outside of work tasks, and you may be surprised that not only are you more relaxed, but you somehow end up being more productive anyway. Let's look more closely at some of the underlying principles that create this fundamental shift in attitude.

You don't have to work first before you can enjoy your life.

The myth is that you work and then reward yourself afterward with an enjoyable, guilt-free life. If you are having a good time, resting or playing before your work is done, you're being like a naughty child and feel bad. Therefore, procrastinators feel ashamed and worthless and are unable to enjoy their downtime even when not working.

To follow this approach, you need to commit to prioritizing play. Notice when you feel guilty or anxious. Remind yourself that play and rest are *part of* being an effective human being entirely, as well as more effective at your work. It's not weak or self-indulgent to enjoy your life. In fact, guilt and obligation may make it much harder to be productive. You deserve to rest—yes, even now, before you've completed the ever-increasing list of tasks on the to-do list. The psychology of this approach is about taking a kinder approach to rest and play—as well as to work. It's not some terrible burden. Flip the standard narrative on its head and you actually give yourself the privilege of seeing that work can be really enjoyable; you build up an unconscious desire to work more.

Turn your to-do list upside down.

Unschedulers don't have a list of tasks. Rather, they add a task to their schedule only after they've actually been doing it for at least 30 minutes. Perhaps you can already see the built-in psychological challenge and motivation in doing it this way around. With a timebox, you could realistically spend 30 minutes dithering and working inefficiently because unconsciously you're waiting for the clock to run out. But this way around, you may find yourself more motivated—and ultimately putting in more time when you do sit down to work.

Better yet, a record of achievements you've already "banked" feels so much better emotionally than a list of all the things you *should* do. You get a tangible feeling of having achieved something. You watch the time available on your schedule filling up with good stuff and feel inspired to do even more. A far cry from procrastination! So block in the time you log after 30 minutes and really stop to appreciate the work you've done. Be proud and internalize those good feelings by writing them down or sharing your results with trusted others. That guilt you feel at the end of the day for doing "nothing"? Well, now you have hard evidence otherwise. Create a positive feedback loop by only focusing on what you have done, not on what you haven't.

Importantly, you're going to need to watch for distractions. You want at least 30 minutes, but 30 *undisrupted* minutes. You might notice that so-called "deep work" takes less overall time but is far richer and of better quality. With time, you may see that you'd rather do 30 minutes of good, solid work and then an hour of play or rest or anything else instead of 1.5 hours forcing yourself through a task you don't want to do and being distracted every five minutes anyway. Try to work for longer patches of time, fully engaged, with zero distractions, pushing the limits of your cognitive capacity (remember flow?). You'll extract more productivity and satisfaction from less time, leaving you with more of your life to enjoy as you like, guilt-free.

Avoid mentally and emotionally draining "shallow work" where you keep busy, watch the clock, flit from one distraction to the next, and then feel bad when you stop, unable to rest because you know that your break time is disappearing with every second and you have to return to work again. It's what makes you feel like you've been "busy" all day with nothing to show for it. It leaves you feeling emotionally tired but not really mentally stimulated and with a heap of negative feelings toward your work. Is it any wonder we procrastinate?

As you can see, the unschedule approach is more about tackling the emotional aspects of work and why we avoid it. It's more about the *why* of procrastination than the *how*—if you're someone who has identified primarily psychological or emotional reasons for your procrastination habit, this approach may work where plenty of other more practically oriented techniques fail. On the other hand, this approach may not work as well if your issue is more that you're cognitively overwhelmed, confused, or simply don't know how to start or organize yourself.

If you find unscheduling works for you though, stick with it. It's all about creating those positive associations with work and building up an unconscious desire to optimize, to really create value. This will loosen the grip of any bad procrastination habits as well as enriching the work you do. Take the time to reward yourself if you succeed in sitting down at a task for more than 30 minutes. Tell your brain to focus on this feeling of satisfaction and pleasure by recording your achievement or rewarding yourself with some play or rest or a more enjoyable task.

Overcoming inertia takes effort. Paying focused attention takes effort. Remember that "behavior that gets rewarded gets repeated" and "what gets measured gets improved." Rather than associating your work with dread and guilt and obligation, you begin to associate it with some pretty powerful feelings of confidence and achievement. Your schedule stops being a slave driver and becomes a record of your achievements and progress, so it's important to log what you've done. Look back on this log at the end of every week or month.

Rest and relaxation are important.

Let's turn to the "day off" principle. Using Fiore's guidelines, take one full day off every week, at least, to tackle little errands, relax, or simply enjoy yourself. If you feel guilty doing so, look at the reason why. Are you still laboring under the belief that you're not allowed to enjoy life until your work—which is never realistically finished—is finished? When you relax, remind yourself that you are lowering your chances of procrastination, resentment, and burnout later down the line.

And really, relaxation time has so many more benefits than merely recharging your batteries so you can go out to work and drain them again. Time spent enjoyably adds dimension, meaning, and color to your life. It *is* your life. Think of it this way: an overachiever, workaholic, and perfectionist is just as bad as an underachiever and procrastinator. They both mismanage their time, energy, and emotional health.

Instead, keep balanced. Protect your vacation time like it's as vital and nonnegotiable as your yearly dental check-up—because it is. It's the old quality versus quantity argument. Wouldn't you rather take appropriate time off and allow yourself to *build up* a store of fresh energy and enthusiasm for work than continually *drain* an already empty tank and force what little you can from yourself, physically, emotionally, and even spiritually?

Take at least a day off per week and at least an hour a day for simple relaxation. Start to reframe this as your responsibility. It is not morally wrong to stop working or to "do nothing." Be careful, also, that you're not approaching your downtime with the same attitude you bring to work. Pushing yourself through leisure activities just because you believe you *should* is counterproductive. In fact, stop thinking of it as "downtime" at all—it's not time defined as the absence of work, but the presence of other wonderful things you care about and that are good for you.

Are you worried you'll end up being a lazy good-for-nothing who never gets the job done? Another rule for managing your time and energy is to commit to 30 minutes of work before doing a social engagement or activity. Yes, it is somewhat the "work before play" mindset, but you're in charge. Here, you focus on the reward, on deep work, and ensuring you enjoy your leisure time without guilt. It's a way to spread a little of your enthusiasm for one activity onto another.

Just start, keep starting, and never end "down."

Don't worry about finishing. Forget the goal for a second. Just start. Then keep just starting, over and over. Keep your eye on the small tasks only—think process, not outcome. Finally, stop a task on a good note. End when you're ahead, in other words, and don't stop in the middle of a challenge, otherwise you give yourself something unpleasant to pick up when next you start. If you can, leave yourself a nice little nugget of fairly pleasant work to wait for you at your next work session—this makes it easier to start again.

Diet Time

With both of these techniques, it becomes very clear how you are spending your time. It's important to draw a distinction that some of us fall prey to—information consumption and diminishing returns.

Consuming information is almost always seen as a net positive. It's what we believe underlies being educated and intelligent, and reading in particular is seen as superior to more passive forms of media consumption.

The point is that it's easy to feel like we're being productive by reading, when all we're actually doing is wasting time in a slightly more intellectual way than binge-watching *Game of Thrones*. When we justify our information consumption in this way, what we're really doing is justifying our procrastination. We use information as a procrastination tool. Reclaim your lost time and get started by going on an *information diet*.

Information diets aren't about being less educated or cutting out leisure reading; they're simply about considering our end goals and if we are unconsciously doing something detrimental to those goals. Too often and too easily, we get *sucked into* information, and when we consume, we cannot do.

But how do we decide what information is worth consuming and what's worth leaving on the shelf? How do we even know what information is sucking up our time? Begin by taking an honest look at how you spend your time. You can do this in the following steps.

1. Survey your information consumption.
2. Remove at least 50 percent of the least valuable content you consume and cut the noise from your information diet.
3. View descriptions of information pieces as pitches for your time and attention.
4. Say no more often.

5. Consider cutting entire information forms from your life.
6. Monitor how much of any one information source you're consuming.

For one week, make a list of every type of media you consume, from your Facebook feed to *War and Peace*.

It's important to know exactly where your time is going so you can make cuts. You might be surprised to find you're scrolling through social media feeds for hours per day, or you may discover that you spend far too many hours inhaling the latest bestseller. It doesn't matter what you're consuming when you begin this process; what matters is that you identify where your time is going so that you can redirect it toward activities that need to get done.

After you make your list, you'll see a lot of different mediums. Social media, books, magazines, television, podcasts, and similar items will probably populate your list. Some are genuinely valuable; they help you be more creative, bring you joy, and make you and your life better. They assist you in your work, or they are flat-out required research to keep you progressing and growing. This doesn't all have to be edifying; genuinely enjoying a TV show or other product can be a good enough reason to keep it in your life.

But right off the bat, you can also see that some of these are useless and keep you stuck in inaction. You'll find a lot of items that you didn't actively choose to watch or read; they were just there, in front of you, and you consumed them on autopilot. Autopilot as unconscious consumption is the real enemy here.

You can tell something should be cut out of your life when it has no current or practical utility. Only information we can immediately apply to our current situation is important. This is what happens when we fall into the Wikipedia rabbit hole, for instance—suddenly we end up learning about 17th-century woodworking when we were only trying to become knowledgeable about one historical figure.

Hypothetical or *just in case* information can also be useful, but most of the time it shouldn't be your current focus. This is like researching the type of clothing you should buy when you lose 50 pounds—it's a legitimate concern, but not at the present moment.

Once you cut out 50% of the least useful media you consume, you'll have that much more spare time to devote to the things you've been putting off. That's way better than wasting time skimming through posts or blankly watching a show you don't care about. This tactic in itself isn't a cure for procrastination, but it does help when you are at the fork in the road, and if a distraction is less handy, it's one less obstacle to working.

It helps to view television, books, articles, and podcasts as pitches for your time and attention. Both are finite; everything we consume also consumes our time and energy. In addition, we can't produce at the same time as we're consuming. It's impossible to do both at once.

At this point, it should be obvious that being entertained or educated doesn't come free of cost, even when no money is being charged. Even when items are free, they're not without cost to your work and productivity.

In addition to considering the inherent cost of consuming information, there's a much simpler way to change our habits: commit to saying no. Merely deciding to stop indulging in media a set number of times, say three times per week, can radically change how we interact with the world.

Without consciously setting limits, it's easy to see keeping up with friends on social media as an obligation or to feel like we have to finish watching the show we like, but none of that's compulsory. At all points, we control our action. We can always say no.

Finally, consider how much time you're sinking into all the remaining forms of media you consume. How much time is spent on television, reading, listening to podcasts, or scrolling through feeds? If you spend too long in any one place, it's likely you're devoting time to those activities because they're automatic, not because you're really enjoying them. Cutting back in those areas can leave more time for the good things in life.

Learning to make cutbacks on attention expenditures lets us focus on information that helps us grow, learn, and thrive. Fortunately, the process of reducing the noise from your media streams can be approached in many ways, allowing anyone to make small—or even major—changes in their routines.

Takeaways:

- A schedule can be just a schedule in the way that a hammer can be just a hammer. But why not use it to its greatest potential instead of as something you only take out for passive purposes? Scheduling is powerful because it very clearly sets out our intentions and goals often on a daily or hourly basis. So why aren't we using them more? In this chapter, we lay out two divergent methods of using a schedule: timeboxing and unscheduling.

- Timeboxing is all about living in your calendar. Whatever is on your mind needs to be scheduled first and foremost. In this way, a calendar is a commitment device that keeps you on track, and organized as well, because timeboxing involves accounting for time, environment, context, energy, desire, and difficulty. It really is as simple as devoting yourself to a schedule and making sure that nothing falls through the cracks. It turns out that when we set out our intentions, we tend to keep them more often than not.

- Unscheduling is the radical opposite because it takes the focus off of work. In some ways, it is more realistic, because it dictates that you fill in your schedule with all of your nonnegotiables and life priorities. That way you can see how much time you actually have to work and think. It also allows you to see what is missing from your life and is harming you emotionally. Work comes last in this type of schedule, which is a weird thing to desire, but unless we have emotional energy and psychological comfort, then we will never get around to our tasks anyway, right?

- Paying more attention to your schedule and daily actions will result in some self-awareness and clarity about how you are spending your time. One thing to pay specific attention to is how much information you consume and at which point you are hitting the point of diminishing returns. As it turns out, much sooner than you might think, so you should consider going on an information diet and cutting out many of the sources of pure information in your life. They aren't doing you any good; they are probably mostly automatic behaviors that suck up your time and mental bandwidth.

Chapter 4. A Return to the Humble "To-Do" List

Having considered so many of the reasons that we procrastinate and the different approaches we can take to undoing this habit and getting back on track with the tasks that will lead us to our dreams, it's time to take another look at that old organizational classic: the to-do list. It hardly needs an introduction. By making a list, you keep track of what needs to be done, you reward yourself when you do it, and you have a log of what has already been done, often using nothing more than a pen and paper. You make sure that nothing slips through the cracks, and you can carry on item by item in an orderly fashion. Even if you're just writing tasks down on a Post-It to remember for later, you're using a form of to-do list and reaping the benefits. As it turns out, there are many variations to this simple theme.

Of the methods we've discussed so far, this one arguably actually has the most to do with psychology. Essentially, it's a technique that works with your brain's inbuilt reward system via the neurotransmitter dopamine. The principle is simple: when we get something we want—a promotion, an ice cream cone, a kiss from a loved one—our brain releases dopamine. It's called the "feel good" hormone because it does just that: makes you feel good, want more, and seek it out continually.

If you can work with, instead of against, this very basic mechanism, you can make it so that you enjoy and *want* to do those tasks that might ordinarily make you procrastinate. Make a list. When you cross that item off, you get a little rush of dopamine and feel a flutter of achievement and progress. You associate the task with pleasure. Result? You're more likely to do that task, or one like it, again. By tethering a task to this good feeling, you're associating your work with pleasure, making it more likely you'll do it. It's really that simple, but this type of addictive tendency applies to all things in our lives, good and bad.

If you've battled "screen addiction" or distractions in your work, you probably already know that it's because all those activities have become recognized by your brain as sources of dopamine release. If you can make doing your to-do list as enticing and pleasurable as the notification alert sound on your phone, perhaps you'd get addicted to doing your chores instead!

Of course, there's no special magic in the list itself—it's what the list represents. The release of dopamine accompanies feelings of accomplishment, pride, release, and progress. It's so satisfying that we want to repeat the experience. Will it work for tasks you truly dislike, though? Actually, you might find that these work even better for those tasks—after all, the sense of accomplishment is greater. You just have to make sure that you can tick boxes frequently enough to keep the dopamine flowing.

Some people even find that knocking off mundane chores from a to-do list becomes empowering, stress-relieving, and deeply satisfying. After a stressful day at work, for example, where nothing went right, it might actually be therapeutic to come home and obliterate your cleaning list, giving yourself those much-craved feelings of efficacy, completion, and achievement.

How can you use the dopamine-power of to-do lists to their best? This even works with the most mundane of to-do lists, though we will delve into specific types soon.

First of all, squeeze as much from them as possible by making the tasks small for the highest number of dopamine "hits." Again, we see why it's so important to break a task down into manageable chunks. As you cross something off the list, really take the time to savor that sense of satisfaction. Clearly and deliberately obliterate it from the list; bask in the sense of accomplishment and reward. There's a reason some people don't just tick an unpleasant item from their list but scratch it out ferociously with a pen like they're killing it! Oh, it feels so good.

A different but related effect is the *Zeigarnik effect*, named after the psychologist who first described it in the late 1920s. She noticed that busy waiters could juggle complex orders in a restaurant, but as soon as the order was fulfilled, they promptly forgot that information. It was as though unfinished tasks were naturally more prominent in their minds than tasks that were already finished. And in fact, it was and continues to be true about our brains— that which is hanging or pending will stick in our minds more readily than something that we deem complete.

Though it seems obvious, what Zeigarnik noted was that the brain will always prioritize and focus on what it perceives as an outstanding task. She found in her research that, if people were interrupted mid-task, they remembered the details of the task far better than if they were asked to remember details about it after they'd already completed it. In other words, uncompleted tasks are better remembered.

Essentially, if you have outstanding uncompleted tasks, they'll stay more prominently in your mind, and that nagging feeling will push you to attend to them. By writing a to-do list, you are drawing even more attention to those things that have yet to be finished, enhancing the pleasure you get from actually doing them when you do and increasing your ability to be productive and effective until then. Use this effect to your advantage: don't multitask since this leaves too many anxiety-causing unfinished projects on your mind, diminishing your focus on the main task. Write essential tasks down, where they'll quietly "nag" at you until they're done. Perhaps this is why a 2013 study by Hammadi showed that consumer attention can so easily be manipulated when this effect is used in advertising—only there, the nagging can only be quieted by making a purchase.

An interesting 2006 study showed that this effect is undermined whenever you expect to get a reward. Eighty-six percent of participants who were interrupted mid-task were eager to continue the task when they didn't know there would be a reward at the end, whereas just 58% of participants who had been told about a reward wanted to. The participants who expected a reward actually spent less time on the activity. What this suggests, contrary to our conventional understanding, is that dangling a future reward off in the distance actually *decreases* our chance of doing a task and doing it well.

Knowing this, it might make sense to make sure you're getting your dopamine hit at the right time so that you're incentivizing yourself to complete a task rather than disengaging because the "reward" has already been experienced. Practically speaking, don't be tempted to tick items off the list prematurely. Some people believe that announcing grand plans before you've taken action toward realizing them has the same effect—in announcing your goal, you get a brief flash of dopamine akin to actually having completed the task and are therefore less inclined to actually do it.

To-Do Lists on Steroids

Time to be honest about your to-do list, if you have one. If yours is mostly left uncompleted at the end of each day, is packed full of vague (i.e., not smart) goals, or overall makes you feel *less* organized, you need an update. Again, let's remember that the list itself is nothing special—it's what it represents. A list needs to be focused, relevant, and achievable. It needs to work, and there are multiple ways to be strategic in how you organize it. What works for one person may not work for another; in the end, it doesn't really matter which method you choose.

One way to de-bloat a to-do list that's gotten too long for its own good is to simply ignore everything except a maximum of three tasks per day—make sure to list out smaller subtasks that fall under those three larger tasks to get the ball rolling for yourself. You tackle these first and foremost, and you list everything else under the "nice to do" category. Even if at the end of the day some items remain undone, you get the satisfaction of knowing your most important tasks were completed. We have a limited amount of energy each day, so spending it on the most important tasks you've identified could make sense. It turns out that many tasks that we think are important can afford to be pushed or postponed without any negative effects— this is something we'll cover later when we talk about the Eisenhower Matrix. And of course, with only three items, there is something motivating about actually accomplishing what you set out to do for a day instead of only chipping away at an enormous list that makes you feel like Sisyphus pushing the boulder up a hill.

Other people like to look at the day ahead holistically and set an intention for what they want to achieve *overall*. It may be something like "Today I'll commit to facing my challenges head-on and calmly," or it could be "By the end of the day I want to feel more in control of this project and a bit clearer on the way forward," and so on. This could manifest as a tangible, quantifiable result ("I want to have read these five chapters by the end of the day") or not. That's up to you. Call it a mission of the day, which then ends up setting the tone for all the tasks to follow.

With the sole intention and mission spoken into reality, it's time to think about the to-do list that supports them. Bearing the Pareto principle in mind (focus on the 20% of the work that gives 80% of the results), try to narrow your list into two larger tasks and three smaller tasks. Larger tasks will take up to two hours to complete, while smaller tasks will take up to 30 minutes to complete.

Intentionally limit yourself to those five task slots a day—this also sets an upper limit on your workload of roughly 5.5 hours a day. Depending on your context and capacity, you can also create nine slots overall: one large task, three medium tasks, and five small tasks. This will still provide focus and intention while limiting the number of tasks on your plate.

These limitations truly force you to cut down on overwhelming feelings and force you to think about what's really important and what is really leading to your intention and mission. It's like you've set a deadline for yourself, which means that you can't dillydally or squander time like you normally would. So take a while to identify each task and get an idea of why you're doing it, what's needed, and how long it will take. If you're timeboxing, schedule these items, building in ample room for breaks and an opportunity to appraise and adapt as necessary. If you're "unscheduling," commit to finding the flow for at least 30 minutes and go from there.

From here, we go slightly backward: how do you actually decide what's most important and what is a big or small task? When you have many different things that need to get done, it can be difficult to know where to start. To succeed with your to-do list, you'll need a way to determine which projects should come first and which can wait. And in fact, assigning value and weighting your to-do list becomes another type of method in itself. One of the most popular ways to do this is to rate using three metrics: seriousness, urgency, and growth. Seriousness speaks to how important the task is, urgency notes how soon the task is due, and growth describes how quickly the problem will get worse if it isn't handled immediately. These metrics place your tasks into the real world and look at consequences.

Rate your tasks on a scale of 1–5 for each category and see how things shake out. You might be surprised. An additional factor might be to analyze the amount of time each task takes. Now you truly have a dynamic to-do list that is more helpful than a series of bullet points.

Categorize Tasks

Again, a straightforward to-do list can be just as unproductive as having nothing at all. It can make you spin your wheels, create anxiety, and cause more confusion than it should. After finishing a task, you can very easily slip into the danger pit that arises when you attempt to select your next task, creating a loss of focus.

This occurs if you only list every task you need to complete without priority or organization. If you've got a to-do list that simply lists 10 tasks, how do you even know where to start? Do you start from the top and work your way down to the bottom? What if you start in the middle? What if you get stuck on the first task? You can spend 10 minutes trying to make sense of your task landscape every time you glance at it, or you can use categories to effectively milk the most from your list.

A list for a list's sake doesn't accomplish everything you need it to in an efficient way; it only ensures you don't forget tasks completely. Of course, this is valuable in itself to reducing your stress and anxiety, but we are striving for more than that. Break your to-do list into categories that will let you know exactly how to spend each minute of your day.

Here are the five categories I suggest for your to-do list on steroids. They are ordered from top to bottom in terms of priority—because that's what matters. This is how you squeeze productivity out of every waking minute. The categories work sequentially; only when you feel that you're done with the prior category should you move onto the next.

Category One: Immediate Attention

Immediate attention—well, that's self-explanatory, isn't it? Check this one first and stay here until it is empty. These are the tasks that you must do that day or even every hour. There might be deadlines associated with them, either internal or external.

Order tasks within this category from most urgent to least. This is the first category to address when you look at your to-do list. Everything else for the day is just a bonus and nice to have. In fact, you should block everything else out until these items are completed because nothing else matters. Don't look at the other categories until your *Immediate Attention* items are done.

Within this category, you should order the tasks from most urgent to least. This is where the essential work is and where you should focus your efforts.

For a teacher, *Immediate Action* items might be grading homework assignments or writing a test to be given the very next day. Things for the following week can be ignored and put off until later.

Category Two: In Progress

These are tasks you have been working on or that might be longer-term in nature. They are not urgent. *In Progress* items are for all intents and purposes what you were planning to begin your day with, except for the fire drill of the *Immediate Attention* tasks.

You may not be able to finish them that day or hour, but you should check in to see how they are progressing *after* you've attended to your most urgent *Immediate Attention* items. These are also items that might need incremental work every day, so make sure to meet your daily responsibility to them.

These tasks won't make it into the *Immediate Attention* category because they can't be accomplished in one day or sitting, so their urgency is lower. Still, this should be the second category you check to make sure that long-term or frequent projects are indeed moving along as they should. Often, these appear to be more important than they are because they are always present. But don't let that fool you—there will likely be no quick consequences for missing these items.

For a teacher, *In Progress* items might be monitoring grades, dealing with emails from parents, or organizing a field trip for next week. These are all things that need to occur on a regular basis, but they can always slide down in priority when urgent matters come.

Category Three: Follow-Ups

These are items that aren't necessarily in your control, but you need to check up on them to make sure they are moving along. This category is outward-facing and focused on corresponding with others and checking on tasks in motion. Most of the time, your emails and calls can be pushed down to this level of priority. This is an especially frustrating category because it feels like you should be doing something about them, even though there is nothing to do. The items in this category feel mentally unfinished, and they unfortunately occupy a space in your brain.

Things you might list here are to remind others about something, to follow up on a project, or to call someone back. This is also where you take note of tasks about which you have not heard back. In a sense, this is similar to the "don't do" list—they are not your responsibility, and you don't have to actively do anything besides check in with people.

This category is mainly for checking the progress of tasks that have made it out of the prior two categories. If they have been stalled on something unrelated to you, your job still isn't done yet! Even so, these don't warrant a higher priority because the main focus isn't on you. You just want to make sure they will be ready for you when you need them.

For a teacher, *Follow-Up* items might be making sure all permission slips have been signed and organizing a teacher's luncheon is on track. None of these rest on the teacher himself at the moment, but they *involve* him overall.

Category Four: Upcoming

The *Upcoming* tasks are a category you want to keep your peripheral vision on. These are things that might be tomorrow or next week, or they might depend on the current tasks you are finishing up now.

Whatever the case, they aren't things you should currently devote your time to. They are the next dominos to fall, and what you should proactively plan for so you have a clear idea of what the rest of your week or month looks like. This category is about setting yourself up for the future versus doing something for the present moment.

It's a good idea to plan out your *Upcoming* tasks as far ahead of time as possible and simply be aware of what's going to be on your docket on any given day or week. This ensures you don't miss anything by constantly thinking about what your next steps are. What will you need to focus on once your current docket is clear, and what kind of urgency will those items require once they become current?

This is the category of tasks that people can most stand to improve on. We all know what tasks are urgent and require our primary and secondary efforts, but what about what follows? Focusing more attention to this category will help you maintain better focus in the long run.

For a teacher, *Upcoming* items might be thinking ahead to group projects for the next unit and projecting when you will run out of construction paper. These won't come into play for days, if not weeks, but understanding what's to come is important in pacing and focus.

Category Five: Ideas

This category should resemble more of a list of ideas and tasks that you want to explore. They are aspirational. It might say something like "Phone as a memory recorder?" These are ideas that you can't devote time to immediately and are therefore your last priority, but you still need to keep them in mind.

Take notes on your future projects whenever you can and they will take shape sooner rather than later. These ideas will often start as big-picture tasks and then break down into small, manageable chunks and tasks. You might spend a lot more time here than you think because nothing else can actively be worked on at the moment. Remember, that doesn't mean nothing is happening; it's just that your role is paused for the time being.

This category is about planning for the future and long-term success. If you have extra time, this is something you can work on developing, but not until the rest of the categories are accounted for—those are higher priorities to take care of and manage. *Ideas* is the last category you check. It's a luxury to be able to reach this category. It allows a level of thoughtfulness and attention that we tend to ignore.

For a teacher, *Ideas* items might be researching next year's curriculum and new ideas for class field trips. Getting into the habit of brainstorming new ideas and areas for improvement is certainly going to set this teacher up for success.

Remember, the objective of categorizing your to-do list is to cut down on the mental effort involved in thinking, "What should I be doing right now?" It gives you a clear blueprint as to where your efforts are needed.

If it takes you 5–10 minutes every time you look at your list to figure out where you should be, that's a massive inefficiency that needs to change. If you institute categories, you'll know exactly what you should be doing at any minute of the day with just a quick glance.

Upgrade Your To-Do List with the Q2 Matrix

Sometimes called the Eisenhower box, and sometimes the Covey Quadrant (after *7 Habits of Highly Effective People* author Stephen Covey, who popularized the idea), the table below is a simple but powerful tool to kick your to-do list into shape. We'll call it the Q2 matrix of our purposes.

URGENCY

	HIGH	LOW
HIGH	**Q1** Strategy: Just do it. Example: House on fire	**Q2** Strategy: Schedule it. Example: Exercise
LOW	**Q3** Strategy: Delegate/Push Back Example: Someone else's urgent deadline	**Q4** Strategy: Don't do it. Example: Refiling last year's important documents

IMPORTANCE

One of the premises is that different activities on your daily schedule are not all going to be of the same order and so shouldn't be treated the same way. We all know the importance of prioritizing, but the Q2 matrix gives you a method for *how* to decide what gets prioritized.

It's simple: every activity falls into one of the four quadrants, according to two features: urgent or not urgent and important or not important. Determine where each task falls on both of those axes and you give yourself a framework to rank and organize your tasks.

Let's start with Q1 tasks—those activities that are both urgent and important. This is called *the Quadrant of Necessity,* since, naturally, getting these tasks done is essential for your life and work. It's not necessarily that these tasks will massively advance your grandest dreams and plans, but rather that *not doing* them will have a steep cost. Anything that's on a deadline and crucial for the functioning of day-to-day life falls in this category—for example, filling a chronic medication prescription or submitting an important project when it's due.

Q2 tasks are in the *Quadrant of Extraordinary Productivity* and are important but not urgent. These are all those tasks that are vital for your well-being and the execution of your life's bigger goals and plans, but there's no rush to do them right now, and if necessary, they can be deferred a little. However, these tasks are still very important. By working on these high-quality activities, you bring yourself closer to your goals, making the best use of your time. Examples include reading and meditating, focusing on quality time with loved ones, self-care, journaling and organizing, learning a new skill or instrument, or adding a little bit of work to a long-term project.

The Quadrant of Distraction, Q3, are those things that are not important but urgent. Actually, in most cases it just *seems* like they're urgent, in the way that distractions, addictions, anxieties, and interruptions often do. In essence, Q3 tasks can masquerade as Q1 tasks and waste your time and energy. How can you tell the difference? Q3 tasks will not be coherent with your own, internally derived goals and values (i.e., not really important). Someone knocking on your door and asking you to sign a petition about an issue you don't care about is a Q3 task. In the moment, you may feel pressured to act, to make a decision, or to hand over your attention. It may be a question of pressure or obligation from others. These tasks can be identified by the fact that they're not genuinely important to you, and not genuinely urgent either, although they may feel like it.

Finally, Q4 is the *Quadrant of Waste*—that is, all those things that are neither important nor urgent. In other words, these are tasks to avoid entirely when possible. For example, browsing online forums for hours is not important in the grander scheme of your life happiness, and it's certainly not urgent. We can see most clearly with Q4 activities that this system is subtle and that tasks should be understood in context. For example, if a moderate amount of gaming actually helps you connect with your community and leaves you feeling relaxed, you may list it as a Q2 activity. At the same time, gaming for eight hours straight and forgoing a shower will push the activity into the Q4 quadrant.

What we can see, essentially, is that ultimately you have to decide honestly and accurately what is "important" in your life and whether it's a real or imagined sense of urgency. To make the Q2 matrix work, you'll also need to be familiar with your life goals and values, otherwise you'll have no standard against which to assess each activity.

So how do you put this Q2 matrix into practice?

Firstly, try doing more Q2 activities every day. Then try to reduce Q1 activities down to the bare minimum—take care of necessities, but don't waste too much time on these tasks. Finally, try to completely eliminate those tasks in Q3 and Q4. Sounds simple, but it could take a while to fine-tune for the unique challenges of your own life.

Master the Q2 quadrant and you'll wind up with days that are filled with the maximum number of value-adding, life-enriching activities, the bare essentials taken care of, and few to no activities that only waste your time, energy, or money. In the process, you boost your productivity, but also your sense of personal fulfillment, self-determination, and efficiency.

Your focus every day should be on Q1 and Q2 tasks. Do the Q1 tasks and then spend time maximizing the Q2 tasks. There are different ways to do this. You could start out by drawing up a to-do list and then going over each item, asking how important and urgent it is. Identify the Q1 tasks, and if you like, rank them. This focuses you and has the effect of cutting down on overwhelm. Your Q1 list is always going to be smaller, and you know that in completing these tasks, you ease time pressure and get out of "survival mode." In reality, very few of us have more than three genuine Q1 tasks every day. Use what you know about your energy levels and the resources you have at hand to decide which tasks to tackle first, then do them as quickly as possible.

Now, here comes the subtle art of using the Q2 matrix for your own benefit. Many people will feel like their whole lives are just wall-to-wall Q1 activities, and when they get a spare moment, they give in to Q4 activities to "relax," while their dreams and goals go unfulfilled. In a way, Q1 tasks are their own kind of distraction, and the world of what's "necessary" can feel like it arbitrarily expands all the time. Think of the matrix as a budget not for time or money, but for energy and intention. The sad truth is that it takes conscious effort to pursue those activities that deliberately advance your position. If you do nothing to help that process along, your life *will* get eaten up by necessities and distractions.

Applying the Q2 framework on your to-do list for a few days will show you where your energy is actually going every day, and this can give you real insight. For the first few weeks, you might find yourself purposefully demoting some Q1 tasks and forcing yourself to do the Q2 tasks. In the long run, it's the accumulation of these Q2 tasks that will improve your life, while the Q1 tasks merely allow it to tick along without incident. You'll have to experiment a little to find your ideal balance. You might choose one day to defer or delegate a Q1 tasks so that you can spend time with family, rest, or take care of your mental and physical well-being. You may find in practice that the only real difference between Q1 and Q2 activities is some creative time management—Q2 activities are those that must be done, and Q1 activities are those that must be done *now*.

What about the items on the list you labeled as Q3 or Q4? We've seen that they need to be reduced or eliminated entirely.

Distracting Q3 tasks, for example, can quickly grow out of control and eat up huge amounts of time and energy, often because we falsely believe they're more urgent or important than they are. If *everything* feels important and urgent, that's a sign you lack focus and goal clarity. Without goals of your own, any stimulus or external demand can step in and convince you it needs to be a priority.

Try to actively move some items from Q1 to Q3. Ask whether this task realistically adds to your well-being and goals. Is it *your* necessity or someone else's? Constantly try to shave off those things that add nothing to your life. Many people unconsciously seek out busywork and purposeless activity. Will it make any real difference in a week if you forgo this activity?

Finally, Q4. Waste undermines productivity. Monitor yourself closely to see what effects certain activities have on you. What could be addictive and counterproductive for one person could be healthy and adaptive for another. Only you can decide on what is "excessive." It's not possible to be 100%

free of Q4 activities, but on the other hand, understand that everything in Q4 is taking away time and energy that could go to Q2 activities. Are you willing to sacrifice a few guilty pleasures to achieve what is ultimately more important to you?

The Don't-Do List

After all this talk about Q1 and Q2 thinking, it becomes clear that sometimes we just need to eliminate tasks like we do in Q4. This final section provides another perspective on what to eliminate from your to-do list and thus life.

Too many things have the potential to command our focus, and sometimes we can't differentiate between what we should avoid and what actually deserves our attention. We also may feel that everything is urgent and important. Thus, the focus of this section is to make crystal clear what you should be avoiding.

Now, everyone knows the value of the to-do list. No doubt you've stumbled across tips elsewhere about using a to-do list to increase productivity and your ability to take action. My point is that everyone inherently *kind of* knows what they should be doing and when they need to do it by. The act of writing it down just helps remind them and keep them accountable. This makes them more likely to do what they know they should be doing—more than if they didn't have such a list.

But not everyone knows what they *shouldn't* be doing. Each day, we're faced with trying to figure out what will create the biggest impact for us—and sometimes we spend time we don't have trying to make this choice. Again, we all know the obvious evils to avoid when trying to upgrade productivity: social media, goofing around on the Internet, watching *The Bachelorette* while trying to work, or learning to play the flute while reading.

It can be difficult to distinguish between real tasks and useless tasks, and it will require some hard thought on your part. If you're lucky, you may find that you put almost everything onto your don't-do list, leaving an obvious path for you to take action.

You need to fill your don't-do list with tasks that will sneakily steal your time and undermine your goals. These are tasks that (1) are insignificant, (2) are a poor use of your time, (3) don't help your bottom line or end purpose, and (4) have a serious case of diminishing returns the more you work on them. If you continuously waste your time on these tasks, your real priorities will fall by the wayside. I've identified three general types of tasks to put on your don't-do list:

First are tasks that are priorities, but you can't do anything about them at present because of external circumstances. These are tasks that are important in one or many ways but are waiting for feedback from others or for underlying tasks to be completed first. Put these on your don't-do list because there is literally nothing you can do about them!

Don't spend your mental energy thinking about them. They'll still be there when you hear back from those other people. Just note that you are waiting to hear back from someone else and the date on which you need to follow up if you haven't heard back. Then push these out of your mind, because they're on someone else's to-do list, not yours. The ball is in someone else's court, for better or worse.

Second are tasks that don't add value as far as your main goals and projects are concerned. There are many small items that don't add to your bottom line, and often, these are trivial things—busywork. Do they really require your time? For that matter, are they *worth* your time? These tasks are just wasted motion for the sake of motion and don't really matter in the big picture. This is where we come to differentiating between aimless motion and actual intentional action.

They are easily disguised as each other, right down to the fact that they both feel good to engage in. However, one delivers an outcome that you want (action), and the other is something that doesn't accomplish anything in the end (motion). You can spend a lot of time investigating gyms and researching workout routines, but if you never step foot inside of one, that's a whole lot of wasted motion running on a hamster wheel.

So you should spend your time on bigger tasks that speak to your overall goals and not myopic, trivial tasks. Often, these are useless tasks disguised as important ones, such as selecting the paint color for the bike shed in the parking lot of the nuclear power plant you are building.

Third, include tasks that are current and ongoing but will not benefit from additional work or attention paid to them. These tasks suffer from diminishing returns.

These projects are just a waste of energy because while they can still stand to improve (and is there anything that can't?), the amount of likely improvement will either not make a difference in the overall outcome or success or will take a disproportionate amount of time and effort without making a significant dent.

For all intents and purposes, these tasks should be considered *done*. Don't waste your time on them, and don't fall into the trap of considering them a priority. Once you finish everything else on your plate, you can then evaluate how much time you want to devote to polishing something.

If the task is at 90% of the quality you need it to be, it's time to look around at what else needs your attention to bring it from 0% to 90%. In other words, it's far more helpful to have three tasks completed at 80% quality versus one task at 100% quality.

When you consciously avoid the items on your don't-do list, you keep yourself focused and streamlined. A don't-do list enables you to know exactly where your path should lead and what action to take first. When you're at a fork in the road and each fork looks equally appealing, you're going to be stuck in analysis paralysis (a perpetual debate between options that leaves you motionless in reality). Eliminate some of those forks right off the bat.

Takeaways:

- A to-do list hastily written on a Post-It might be one of the most ubiquitous tools for self-discipline and avoiding procrastination. It works on our psychology by manipulating dopamine, and this is one of the few instances that we can actually make our brains work for us. But ultimately, a to-do list just makes sure that things are not being forgotten or falling through the cracks, and it doesn't necessarily assist you in doing more. It just prevents you from doing *less*. Thus, we need to level up the humble to-do list.
- We can start to do this by trimming the to-do list down to three items per day (yes, only three) to keep focused and lean. We can also set an intention or overall mission for the day and add only five (two big and three small) or nine (one big, three medium, and five small)

tasks to the list in support of that mission. We can also add an element of reality-testing by evaluating your tasks through the metrics of seriousness, urgency, and growth in order to easily see what to prioritize.

- Another way to improve your to-do list is by using categories: immediate attention, in progress, follow-ups, upcoming, and ideas. This allows you to again sort by priority and make sure that you are properly addressing what needs to be addressed.

- The truth is that to-do lists often don't take context into account. Q1 and Q2 thinking solves that problem by forcing you to understand the difference between urgent and important. Most people don't have a grasp of these blurry lines, but it can mean all the difference in your output. Related to this is the don't-do list, also essentially seen in Q4 of the Eisenhower matrix. Most people know what they should be doing but not what they *shouldn't* be doing. This is where you eliminate tasks that (1) are insignificant, (2) are a poor use of your time, (3) don't help your bottom line or end purpose, and (4) have a serious case of diminishing returns the more you work on them.

Chapter 5. Adjust Your Psychology

As you've probably noticed, it's not quite *what* you do when it comes to improving your productivity, but *why* and *how* you do it. No matter which approach you try, keep in mind that you're in charge, and frequently stop to ask whether a technique is working for you. However you keep your to-do list or schedule, keep a record of how many hours you actually do a day, how you feel doing them, and how much time you spend procrastinating. Drop those ideas that aren't working and double down on those that are. Simple—but it does require time and focus.

Let's finish with a few more handy psychological tips and tricks to increase your self-discipline and kill your procrastination habit once and for all. Remember, none of it is gospel—you'll only know if a method has any merit if you take the time to *practically apply* it in your own life. What's important is that you test it out in the real world and make adjustments as necessary.

Coerced Compliance

One useful trick is what's called the Ulysses pact. First, a little story about Ulysses to set the context. In Homer's epic *Odyssey*, Ulysses and his men sail past the notorious sirens, whose beauty and enchanting singing lure men to come closer and kill themselves on the dangerous rocks. It's a metaphor we can all appreciate: the siren song of our most alluring distractions can feel so strong at times we find ourselves behaving completely irrationally and steering off course to our doom.

Ulysses, however, understands that this will happen and decides to take action *while he is still thinking rationally.* On advice of the witch Circe, he tells his men to wear wax earplugs and asks them to tie him tightly to the mast of the ship so that he can hear the song without being physically drawn in (granted, this part is a little cheeky). The sailors manage to resist the pull of the sirens and sail safely by.

From this story, you can probably guess what a "Ulysses pact" might be. We already know that under certain conditions, we don't behave rationally. When a temptation is strong enough, we can't realistically rely on our free will. All our noble commitments and goals fly out the window if a distraction is powerful enough. So don't plan to resist a powerful temptation in the moment—instead, plan ahead and make it so that it's simply *impossible* to succumb to a tempting distraction, no effort required. Harriet Standing and Rob Lawlor at Leeds university discussed in 2019 how this approach can even help with psychiatric patient care, self-harm, addiction, and things like ADHD.

Essentially, you use your rationality and willpower in one moment to bootstrap you through another more challenging moment. By locking yourself into a behavior you set up when you're cognitively and emotionally strong, you avoid a slip later. You don't have to beat yourself up for being a fallible human sometimes who gives in to temptation—simply realize that the possibility is there and act accordingly. Many procrastination and productivity tips focus on building up your strength of will, but why give yourself all that work to do when you can avoid it altogether?

The trick to making this approach really work for you is to create a system (i.e., your own wax earplugs and ropes to tie you to the mast) that will well and truly keep you away from the distraction. The siren song is tempting! An example is to install an app in your Internet browser that blocks you from visiting certain sites. While you are feeling strong, rational, and committed, you set the app to only allow access for a limited period during each day, after you've already done your more important tasks. Thinking ahead, you choose an app that cannot, under any circumstances, be undone. You install the app on all your devices in your home and choose one that cannot be cleverly switched off one way or another. And just like that, the monumental temptation is taken off your plate.

This trick can be used to avoid temptations of all kinds. If you notice that you procrastinate because of ample (technological) distractions, take a moment to think of a system to keep yourself from those distractions when you're feeling in a more in-control mood. Set up your work PC so that it isn't online and you can work in peace without checking mail or browsing endlessly. Give the Wi-Fi password to someone else. Keep games at a friend's house or store your phone in another room overnight so you're not tempted to fiddle with it when you should be sleeping. If you notice that your siren songs are emotional in nature, you may even find it helpful to write yourself a letter in a calm, rational state of mind for you to read later if you get drawn into spirals of negative thinking or pessimism.

Use this technique to not only avoid temptations, but to encourage better habits in the process. A good use of this approach is in getting yourself to eat better. Go grocery shopping when you've already eaten; being full and satisfied will help you resist the siren song of junk food a little better. If you know that the most tempting and unhealthy treats are in the center aisles of the store, commit to only ever shopping on the perimeter where the fresh and unprocessed foods are. Or even better, shop online and get a standard weekly order that takes the choice out of your hands completely. Meal delivery services do the same and will portion your meals and help you avoid going into supermarkets at all.

There are countless ways to use this trick; it all depends on your unique triggers, weaknesses, and reasons for procrastination or other bad habits. A person may find that they have a nasty habit of overeating after dinnertime each evening. They already know how futile it is to try and bravely resist the cookies and candy, night after night. It wears down on their mental reserves and makes them feel bad every time they fail. So they don't bother finding clever ways to resist—they just institute a rule to never have cookies and candy in the house, period. This single decision will remove the need for the near-constant effort of willpower they'd otherwise have to exercise over and over again if these snacks were available.

This is a subtle switch from the behavior we're trying to reduce to the state of mind that causes us to do those behaviors. The fact is that willpower is not limitless and that our ability to continually delay gratification and make the better choice takes effort and energy. This wears down over the course of a day, so you're more likely to make a poor decision if you're already tired. Have you ever told yourself, "What the hell, I deserve this," and indulged at the end of a particularly hard day? It's because, cognitively, you've already "spent" your willpower for the day and it's hopeless to expect that you'd summon it from nowhere to resist the temptation. Instead, give the decision to yourself at your strongest so you can benefit when you're at your weakest.

Consider someone who knows they should be more sociable and cultivate friendships but is lazy and a little socially anxious. Knowing that they tend to flake on social commitments a few hours in advance, they deliberately set up a situation where a friend will come and pick them up and they'll travel together. With the obligation and accountability that comes with this, the person finds they resist the temptation to be lazy and stay home. Granted, they might not *like* it in the moment, but they're probably glad they had the foresight to push themselves anyway.

Similarly, if you avoid the gym and procrastinate going, get an accountability buddy and set up systems that are difficult to wriggle out of. Tell your friend you'll pay them $50 for every workout you miss. Leave something you need for work at the gym lockers so you have to go in before work. Book an appointment with a trainer that you'd feel awkward about canceling.

The important thing is to really understand what your temptations are, how they work, and when they happen so you can step in appropriately. You don't need to pile on guilt when you mess up—bad feelings won't help you one bit when it comes to doing it right. Accept that some temptations are strong, and don't put pressure on yourself to quit things cold turkey or achieve miracles overnight. With some compassion and foresight, you can engineer your day to leverage your more clear, conscious, and inspired moments to get you through your more difficult ones.

The Ulysses pact is just one of many tricks you could use, some of them we've already encountered, and others you might not yet be aware of, such as Kaizen or special techniques for impulse control.

The Master of Discomfort

Ultimately, what we may be looking for when we think about self-discipline is hardening ourselves and gaining the ability to simply push through tasks more often than not.

The brain can be tricked, mindsets can be shifted, and we can manipulate our surroundings all we want. At the core, we still need to engage in something we find at least slightly annoying or uncomfortable. Evidence is everywhere. For instance...

"Lose weight without the diet and exercise!"

"Think positively and you'll get whatever you want, without effort!"

"Follow this plan and you'll only have to work four hours in a week!"

In our modern consumer world, where marketing and advertising compete for our attention and our money at every turn, the name of the game is offering something for nothing. Abs without crunches. Money in the bank without breaking a sweat. Knowledge without studying too hard.

Products like this are successful because they tap into humankind's collective desire to avoid discomfort at all costs. We all have the dream of living in a world where we get everything we want without trying too hard or being scared or making any sacrifice. Otherwise, what's the lottery for?

However, as we've seen, a massive part of success in life comes down to self-discipline, and self-discipline is at its core made of nothing but the willingness to endure discomfort. In other words, there are no shortcuts, no easy life hacks, no quick tricks. Success in the bigger picture belongs to those who have mastered the ability to tolerate a degree of distress and uncertainty and who can thrive in situations of sacrifice in service of something bigger than their immediate pleasure in the moment.

Self-discipline = being uncomfortable. No tips or tactics needed.

We all want to grow and achieve, but the truth is that the state of growth is inherently an uncomfortable one. Evolving feels uncertain and risky at times, and it certainly requires us to give up immediate pleasures and old, easy habits. Growth and development is about expanding, risking, exploring. It cannot be done without leaving the security of the old behind. And sometimes, change requires pain, as the old dies and the new is still small and uncertain.

Self-discipline is not required for the easy parts of life. It takes no effort or special technique to enjoy what we already enjoy. But if we want to productively approach the rest of life, we need to develop the self-discipline to work with the things we don't enjoy. Rather than thinking of pain, discomfort, and uncertainty as roadblocks in our way to pleasure and success, we understand that they're simply a part of life, and if we manage them well, we can unlock even bigger pleasures.

There is a great paradox in learning to not just tolerate but embrace discomfort. Practicing being uncomfortable doesn't sound like much fun, and it isn't. But it is a skill that will reap far more rewards in the long term than merely chasing fleeting pleasures or shifting fancies in each moment.

Simply, we practice self-discipline and familiarity with discomfort because we respect that life contains an inevitable amount of discomfort. We know that in gaining a new perspective on the things we don't really want to do, we actually create new opportunities for fulfillment, meaning, and pleasure. Life becomes easier, and we become stronger, almost larger than the everyday trials and troubles life can throw our way.

With self-discipline, our expectations become healthier and more in line with reality. Our work becomes more focused and purposeful and we are able to achieve more. Self-discipline is not a thing we simply decide we want or think is a good idea in theory. It's a practice that we pitch up for again and again, every day and every moment, willing to work it out in the arena of our lived experience. In other words, self-discipline is a habit in a world where the easiest thing is to take the path of least resistance or fall prey to the "succeed without trying" traps all around us.

It might seem logical at first to pursue pleasure. But if there's one thing we know with utmost certainty, it's that things *will* change around us, we *will* have to endure suffering at one point or another, and we *will* be uncomfortable and forced to face things we wish we didn't have to. If we have this knowledge, isn't it better to be prepared rather than blindly pursue a dazzling goal with no thought to what you'll do when that goal doesn't go how you planned?

Learning how to tolerate distress, uncertainty, doubt, and risk while things are okay (i.e., before these things are forced on you by life) gives you the opportunity to practice and develop your discipline so you're prepared for future discomfort. Yes, it means that walking barefoot makes you more "immune" to one day having to walk without shoes. But it also means you're less attached to needing shoes, and you feel deep down that you are more than able to respond to and endure challenges. This is an attitude of empowerment. It's looking at life's challenges head-on and deciding to accept them and respond with dignity and grit.

Practicing tolerance is a "vaccine" in that you inoculate yourself against future discomfort in general. Adversity will still bother you, but you'll move through it with the quiet confidence that it won't kill you. How can it, when you've endured it all before and only came out stronger?

You can turn your focus to maximizing pleasure and refusing to engage with pain; or you can acknowledge that life intends to serve you heaping doses of both, and if you can prepare with maturity and wisdom, you can stay calm and ride those waves, trusting that you've developed your ability to survive.

So prepare while the going is still easy. Don't wait for life to force you to learn the lessons you must, sooner or later. Take the initiative by developing self-discipline right now. The shift is only a small one, but mentally it has great influence on how you approach yourself and life. The idea is straightforward: get more uncomfortable than you'd usually be. Give yourself the gift of the opportunity to grow stronger.

Importantly, you're not just thinking about these things or talking about them. It's not enough to "get" the concept intellectually or abstractly. One must actually have a *real lived experience* of discomfort. You need to get your hands dirty out there in the trenches of real life.

Develop self-discipline either by putting yourself in uncomfortable positions or by deliberately choosing to forgo comfortable ones. Train your will and discipline in the same way you would any other muscle: with repeated exercise. Become the person that is able to push through and do what others dread doing; become the person who can resist doing what everyone else can't resist. The way to do that? With a finely cultivated ability to tolerate discomfort and forego pleasure.

No, you are not being a masochist. You are not a glutton for punishment who wants to martyr themselves on the personal development altar and make a big show of how poorly they can treat themselves. It is actually your desire for a better, more meaningful life that moves you; it's because you ultimately want to make things easier that you are willing to have them be harder for a while.

Again, the paradox is that deliberately engaging with discomfort sometimes shows you just how insignificant it sometimes is. It allows you to enjoy the pleasures on a richer, deeper level. It's like forcing yourself to look under the bed to check for monsters. In the same way that there never is a monster, self-discipline can also teach you that doing without what you think you "need" is sometimes far easier than we think and that we're far stronger than we believed. Without giving yourself the chance to confront distress head-on, you might always cling to ideas of what you could never endure (i.e., certain the monster is still under the bed because you never gathered the courage to check).

Cold showers, going underdressed for the cold, sleeping on the floor, or foregoing food for a while don't sound like fun, but they are certainly something you can bear. They're all something that you can go through and come out the other end—intact! Afterward, take notice of how you feel. You may be surprised to note a feeling of calm confidence and achievement. Rather than being diminished by the experience, you might feel enriched, in a small way.

You can remind yourself as you endure the discomfort that, with each moment, you are making it more and more likely that you will better cope with adversity in the future. This knowledge gives you confidence and also reduces your fear of the unknown. When you can anticipate a negative outcome and be prepared for it, the future doesn't seem so threatening, and risks seem easier to manage.

You don't want to do any of it, sure. But you can. That's a skill. You *can* take cold showers. You *can* sleep on the floor. You *can* go without food. You *can* bear discomforts when they come. You can proactively manage your own fear and insecurity and get on top of it, rather than have it control you. And better yet, you are better equipped to respond in a world filled with quick fixes, distractions, and easy pleasure.

How does one actually practice all this, though? What does it look like in day-to-day life to cultivate self-discipline?

As a first step, don't dive into the deep end. Build up your confidence and your tolerance bit by bit. Perhaps you decide you'd like to stop mindless distractions like browsing online or looking at your phone constantly. Rather than throwing your phone in a lake and vowing to go offline completely, you instead ratchet up the discomfort slowly, giving yourself time to acknowledge and absorb the feeling of being able to manage. First, you decide not to keep your phone next to your bed. You notice the urge to have it anyway and notice feelings of boredom and the urge to grab it and get that easy dopamine hit.

You tell yourself, "I can do this. I'm in control. It's okay to feel uncomfortable. I'm staying with this feeling of discomfort."

And, lo and behold, you discover you can endure it. You make a habit of it. No arguing, justification, excuses, or avoidance. You simply acknowledge, "Yes, it's uncomfortable. Yes, I don't like it. But that's okay. I can do this."

Next, you inch up the discomfort. You've done the hard work of starting and you've given yourself proof that you can indeed bear discomfort. Now, you can push it a little. Perhaps you decide to whittle your mindless phone scrolling to just an hour a day. It's a small goal, but you achieve it. You feel proud of having done it. You may even notice that this pride feels better than the fleeting moment of entertainment or distraction you got from scrolling in the first place. You keep telling yourself, "I can do this."

Keep going. Gradually push yourself out of your comfort zone. Notice when you're pushing back against your decision. Sit quietly with your discomfort, whatever it looks like. It might take the form of anger or irritation. It might suddenly become very clever and try to convince you how unnecessary this all is and how you might as well cave because it doesn't matter. It might get depressed at having to engage with an emotion it feels entitled to be free of.

Simply watch all this come, and watch it go. Feel the calm you have in the wake of successfully enduring all this discomfort. Isn't it wonderful to know that you can stand calm and strong through the storm? Tell yourself, "It's okay that I'm feeling discomfort. I'm in control. It will pass."

Finally, you might start to notice interesting things happen the more you practice. Watch your discomfort and watch your growing and changing response to it. Are certain things getting easier? Are you becoming familiar with all your idiosyncratic ways of resisting discomfort internally? Say to yourself, "I am capable of sitting with discomfort and any other negative feelings that may pass. I'm watching with curiosity. I will stay here with myself and with the feeling. I can do this. I will not respond with avoidance or escape or resistance. I welcome the experience. I can do this."

Of course, the other side of learning to tolerate discomfort is not just to endure negative feelings but to deliberately put off positive ones. Self-denial is the other side of the same self-discipline coin. Many addictive behaviors have their root in our inability to forego easy pleasure in the moment and bear the reality of the moment just as it is, right now.

Flex your self-discipline muscle by learning to say no to some of your impulses and urges. Train yourself to understand that you can act, even if you don't feel like it, and you can turn down an action, even if you really feel like doing it. As above, give yourself the opportunity to notice the feeling of calm strength this gives you.

Skip eating that sweet treat you go for automatically. Turn off the TV after one episode and force yourself to stand up rather than get sucked into three more episodes. Bite your tongue rather than say something regrettable to someone. A little self-denial opens up a crucial window of opportunity in which you can pause and deliberate on your actions. Are they in line with your ultimate goals? Do you *really* need to do them? What would you gain by turning them down for once?

Self-restraint and presence of mind enhance your sense of empowerment and control. Rather than being reactive and unconscious in your habits, stop and sink into the feeling of not fulfilling every desire, not acting, not going the easy way, or abstaining. It's a counterintuitive approach, but one that only yields greater and greater rewards the more it's practiced.

Here is a brief passage from *Meditations* by the Roman emperor-philosopher Marcus Aurelius that illustrates what we lose by surrendering to discomfort (of which is no concern to him) and not taking steps toward what we want in life:

> At dawn, when you have trouble getting out of bed, tell yourself: "I have to go to work—as a human being. What do I have to complain of, if I'm going to do what I was born for—the things I was brought into the world to do? Or is this what I was created for? To huddle under the blankets and stay warm?
>
> 'But it's nicer here...'
>
> So you were born to feel "nice"? Instead of doing things and experiencing them? Don't you see the plants, the birds, the ants and spiders and bees going about their individual tasks, putting the world in order, as best they can? And you're not willing to do your job as a human being? Why

aren't you running to do what your nature demands?

'—But we have to sleep sometime...'

Agreed. But nature set a limit on that—as it did on eating and drinking. And you're over the limit. You've had more than enough of that. But not of working. There you're still below your quota. You don't love yourself enough. Or you'd love your nature too, and what it demands of you. People who love what they do wear themselves down doing it, they even forget to wash or eat."

Control Your Impulses

One final step toward improving your self-discipline is to learn to control your impulses. They are polar opposites; one is stable and reliable like a metronome, while the other is unpredictable like a volcano.

An impulse is the sudden need to do (or not do) something, an uncontrollable urge. Impulses are often acted upon without forethought or planning and can come out of nowhere to derail your entire day. This is where self-discipline dies, because you are at the mercy of a spur-of-the-moment whim. You can't engage in both at the same time. Control over impulses is a key to consistent discipline.

For instance, imagine that you are playing piano during a big performance, but you get the sudden impulse to scratch an itch on your face. The itch is not urgent, nor is it important, but it's something nagging in the back of your mind that will cause you discomfort unless you address it. Now, will you break your performance to scratch the itch, or will you ignore the temporary distraction? You would probably recognize that your impulse should take a back seat to maintaining self-discipline in this instance.

Only rarely, like the above example, is it clear that we should suppress these random impulses. But just like the piano performance, we don't realize how much indulging in an impulse will throw us off. These things add up, and so does the time required for you to re-focus yourself and get back on the horse of self-discipline.

How can we defeat this type of enemy? First, we must understand it.

Impulses have been the subject of psychological research for many years. Recently, researchers from the European Molecular Biology Laboratory have found strong connections between two parts of the brain related to impulse control: the prefrontal cortex, the part of the brain responsible for complex cognition, personality, decision-making, and social behavior; and the brainstem, the portion of the brain that regulates basic autonomic functions such as heart rate and breathing.

This means that we possess a significant number of connections that allow us to self-regulate and control—it takes a conscious thought in our prefrontal cortex, and it travels to our brainstem for calm and relaxation. When we have a strong link between the two, we can better exercise self-discipline.

However, in the study, scientists found that a condition known as *social defeat* (a negative emotional state) in mice weakened the connection between the prefrontal cortex and the part of the brainstem involved in defensive responses. With a weaker connection, they became more impulsive, wilder, and difficult to calm down. When the researchers used a drug to block the connection between the prefrontal cortex and the brainstem completely, the mice demonstrated even more impulsive behavior.

How does this translate to humans? This research sheds light on what is happening in your brain when you're trying to control an impulse. If we're in an emotional state, the connection between the prefrontal cortex and the brainstem is weakened. We become more impulsive and less self-aware.

We can't very well take drugs to strengthen our neural connections and maintain self-discipline better, but we can try to ensure that our prefrontal cortex is engaged as much as possible. That roughly translates to making decisions based on analysis and rationality versus emotion. Self-discipline won't win in the face of urgency, anxiety, and fear, so you have to let them pass and then keep on keeping on. When we're thinking with our brainstem, which isn't always something we can control, our self-discipline goes out the window.

There are techniques we can implement to help support our desire to better control our impulses. Generally, they involve some sort of delay between feeling the impulse and the reaction you give to it. In other words, the more distance between feeling the itch and scratching the itch, the better. You'll usually find that the impulse simply disappears on its own, which further proves its status as something that is simply masquerading as important (when it's really not).

The power of 10. If you can delay action on your impulses, often you can overcome them. There is something to be said for taking a breath, counting slowly to 10, and giving yourself a moment. Tell yourself to persevere for just 10 more seconds when you want to stop, and tell yourself to try something out for just 10 seconds when you are delaying starting. That's the power of 10—the mere act of holding yourself back requires self-discipline, and you practice feeling a reaction without acting on it.

The power of 10 takes the urgency out of your urge to act immediately. Remember, that's where your brainstem loses its grip over your actions and your prefrontal cortex steps in.

For some impulses, counting to 10 won't suffice. For example, if you see something you want to buy but don't really *need*, instead of just taking it to the register to be rung up, you can take 10 minutes, the second power of 10. This is the same type of diversionary tactic that neuroscientists have found extremely effective to battle impulse-spending and shopping; just 10 minutes drastically reduces the brain's thirsty response for a reward. Rather than rush to purchase the item, you could leave the store for 10 minutes, and you'll be less likely to follow through with the purchase.

Usually, an itch will disappear within seconds. A strong emotional spike will mostly dissipate within 10 seconds. You might stop seeing red in that time span. Your initial reaction just might have given way to rational thought.

After all, anyone can withstand anything for 10 seconds, right? Keep this mantra in mind and bypass the danger zone where your brainstem is in control of your actions.

Label your feelings. A person who doesn't understand his or her emotions is more likely to act on impulse. If you can't identify when you're feeling angry or stressed or embarrassed, you may act in a way that just makes it worse. In essence, if you don't realize what you're feeling, you will be unable to stop it.

For example, suppose you have an argument with someone and you impulsively stomp off and slam the door on your way out. Those behaviors scream anger, but they likely happened so quickly, so impulsively, that you didn't consciously think—you just reacted.

If you took a moment to realize why you want to storm out the door and how angry you are, you would have a better chance of tempering your response. Instead of leaving in a huff, say, "I think I'm feeling angry right now. I should deal with the anger first and then respond after it passes." That takes the acute impulse out of the situation and increases the chance that things will go better once the situation is de-escalated. It also gives you an exact symptom to deal with—anger, resentment, bitterness, frustration—and from that you can find a roadmap to deal with it. That wouldn't be possible without a label.

It's acceptable to feel angry, embarrassed, frustrated, and ashamed. But what *isn't* acceptable is to substitute these initial reactions as your response and act impulsively. When you take a pause to identify what you're feeling, often you will realize that things aren't quite as urgent as you thought.

Write down the facts. Writing down the facts of a situation helps you clarify what is real, what is not, and what your ideal outcome is. This is related to the power of 10 in that you are pausing to sort through the facts before you act impulsively with the brainstem. And of course, you write much more slowly than you think, so this slows your entire reactive process down. That bodes well for the prefrontal cortex and self-discipline.

Thus, when you want to quit something, when you want to delay starting something, or when you suddenly feel an urge to do something unproductive or distracting, write down the facts. Write out what the situation is, what you want to do, and what you should probably do instead. Write down your ideal outcome and how that differs from the path you would take if you gave in to your impulse.

Highlight only what is factual and leave out the rest. Don't write down your feelings, emotions, fears, or anxieties. Keep it black and white. When you have a clear picture of "just the facts, ma'am," you are able to look at the situation objectively and know what you should do. This not only allows you to respond in a more tempered fashion, but it helps you sort out what actually happened versus what you "thought" or "felt" happened.

For example, suppose you had a blow-up with your boss at work, and your impulse is to quit your job and look for a new one. Writing down the facts will help you clarify the situation and sort the emotion from the facts. Maybe the facts are your boss blamed you for a situation; you didn't get to tell your side of the story; you've worked at your current job for eight years; you are the primary breadwinner of your family; in addition to salary, you have good benefits; and you haven't talked to human resources to help resolve the situation. You want to punch his face and quit—that doesn't get you to your ideal outcome. Your ideal outcome involves being heard, being more assertive, and keeping your job.

Suddenly, after taking the time to examine the facts, it's clear what you need to do to maintain self-discipline. An impulse only exists because it is quick and fleeting; under greater scrutiny, they almost all crumble.

Ask "why" five times. A final strategy for helping to control your impulses is asking *why*. This tactic is all about getting to the root of your impulse and hopefully uncovering new information about yourself. You're actually asking the same or similar question five times in a row, and you'll be surprised to learn that each time, you just might pull out a different answer than before. You're forcing yourself to justify why an impulse should win out over self-discipline. At the end of the process, you'll either be able to answer *why* sufficiently, or you'll come to the conclusion that it was simply an impulse not worth partaking in.

Impulses are never thought through or founded on deep analysis, so you wouldn't expect to be able to answer *why* more than once or twice. Thus, only if you can answer *why* a few times does it pass the sniff test of importance or urgency. Practically speaking, what does this look like? Suppose you have an impulse to break your spending discipline and buy a new sweater.

Why do you want it?
I like it.
Why do you want it?
It's a great price. (This is as far as an impulse will probably carry you.)
Why do you want it?
No real reason other than wanting it...
Why do you want it?
Looks cool?
Why do you want it?
I guess I don't, really.

Once you've asked yourself *why* five times, in five different ways, you have distilled the main pros and cons for why you should or shouldn't buy the shirt. And really, you've come up with nothing to justify the impulse. If this was really a shirt that you needed in some way, you'd be able to come up with better answers, such as "Because my other shirt ripped" or "I have a wedding coming up" or "I want to look nice for a date!" In those instances, you are *not* dealing with an impulse masquerading as a need—it's an actual need.

Even if it doesn't bring you to the point where you realize you can't answer *why* five times (which is a red flag), at least it will force you to stop and think about your decisions. Whatever the case, you've become more mindful and more likely to be disciplined in your daily life.

Looking at each of these strategies, the common themes involve reflection, self-awareness, and pausing before responding.

Takeaways:

- The final piece of the puzzle for greater self-discipline and sticking to your guns is to change your thoughts. Thoughts, of course, lead to behavior, and behavior is what we want to change in the end. In this chapter, we talk about three specific ways to change the way that you think about taking action versus lying on the couch.

- First, we come to the Ulysses pact, or as I would call it, coerced compliance. It's the act of burning your bridges and not allowing yourself to make a detrimental choice in the heat of the moment or out of a lack of self-awareness. When you find that you have no choice, and you must actually sit with your thoughts and work through things, that's just what you'll do. There is no easier path of least resistance, and there is no escape. If you can smartly plan and make this choice beforehand using commitment devices such as the Ulysses pact, then you no longer have to exercise self-discipline per se.

- Next, we come to the practice of discomfort and all that it entails. By definition, anything that requires exercising self-discipline is uncomfortable. We'd rather not do it, otherwise it would be known as fun. This puts us in a quandary; sometimes there is nothing else we can do but suck it up and push forward, despite all the tactics and mindsets we've discussed in this book. At some point, we will have to be uncomfortable, and sometimes life is just a matter of how much discomfort you can stomach. Thus, we must practice it, and we will eventually grow immune to an extent. Practicing discomfort is like a vaccine against your impulses and weak moments. When you can slowly gain perspective that discomfort is not so bad and ultimately temporary, you'll be amazed at what you can accomplish.

- Impulses are the polar opposite of self-discipline, and they are things we must consciously train against indulging in. Oh, but it's hard. Impulses are behind every subconscious thought that we struggle to rein in. How can we ever hope to combat this? Generally, we must try to interject space and time between a thought and an action. We can do this by simply counting slowly to 10, labeling your thoughts and feelings, writing down the facts of a situation, and asking yourself *why* five times and making sure to answer honestly.

Summary Guide

Chapter 1. Stop Being So "Lazy"

- When we label ourselves or others as lazy, are we really doing ourselves justice, or is there more to that simple and overused term? What can we learn about simple laziness to defeat it and perhaps set ourselves up for success?

- Laziness is not so much of a cause as it is a symptom of emotional or organizational issues that are present within our mindsets. It's helpful to view these shortcomings as a series of cause-and-effect actions, because the reasons that we are not acting and not exercising self-discipline are more complex than you might realize. We're not lazy; we have many psychological barriers that keep us firmly rooted in place. Take it easy on yourself, because nothing is as simple as "I don't want to do it, so I won't!"

- The main causes for so-called laziness include fear of judgment and negative emotion, fixed mindsets that make action feel useless, organizational issues that keep you confused and spiraling, and physical or mental deficiencies such as sleep, rest, nutrition, illness, and lack of alignment. It's not so much that we need to cure these issues, because that is a tall task without dedicated introspection, but if we are more aware of what drives us to act (or not), then we stand a chance of addressing it on a consistent basis. You may never truly overcome all of those issues, but for our purposes, breaking inertia is the goal.

- In the end, whether we are being "lazy" or not, we are putting what we want at the current moment over what we want the most. We are getting distracted by shiny objects and temporary moments of gratification. And yet, what are we prioritizing at the current moment besides comfort and safety? Are those powerful enough motivators for you to stand between what you want the most? That's a rhetorical question, by the way.

Chapter 2. Formulas for More

- We've gone through some of the psychological beasts that underlie the feeling of "lazy" and it turns out that we are beset by barriers, rather than a preference to be sloths. So what can we do with this knowledge? It doesn't automatically launch us into action, but this chapter is about the second-best thing—providing formulas and workflows of sorts to break down what is missing from action. This way we don't have to feel like we are winging it and instead can follow a set of simple instructions to get things done and exercise self-discipline.
- The first set of instructions comes in the form of Patrick Keelan's flowchart for action. He accurately sees that much of laziness comes from a lack of planning and presence, and his flowchart for action contains four simple steps to move you from Point A to Point B. Action

plan? Are the steps small enough to act upon? Have I used the five-minute rule? Do I have any beliefs or rules keeping me back? Within each of those steps is also the solution to move to the next step of action.

- The second set of instructions comes from Hungarian writer Mihaly Csíkszentmihályi and his flow theory. Flow is about moving and working effortlessly, to the point that you lose track of time and are engrossed in your task. Sounds nice, doesn't it? He lists a set of requirements for achieving flow, but we will focus on the elements of having your actions pointed toward specific goals, a balance of challenge and ease, and feedback to let you know that you are making a difference, thus keeping you motivated toward chasing that feeling.

- Finally, we come to a set of instructions from Piers Steel, dubbed the procrastination equation. He states that motivation = (expectancy + value) / (impulsiveness + delay). First of all, are you even considering each of these four factors when it comes to trying to take action? Are you aware of what's involved? Next, manipulate these motivating factors into a quantity or order that makes the most sense for you. You'll quickly find what helps your sense of self-discipline, a term that, like "laziness," has several layers to it.

Chapter 3. The All-Powerful Schedule

- A schedule can be just a schedule in the way that a hammer can be just a hammer. But why not use it to its greatest potential instead of as something you only take out for passive purposes? Scheduling is powerful because it very clearly sets out our intentions and goals often on a daily or hourly basis. So why aren't we using them more? In this chapter, we lay out two divergent methods of using a schedule: timeboxing and unscheduling.
- Timeboxing is all about living in your calendar. Whatever is on your mind needs to be scheduled first and foremost. In this way, a calendar is a

commitment device that keeps you on track, and organized as well, because timeboxing involves accounting for time, environment, context, energy, desire, and difficulty. It really is as simple as devoting yourself to a schedule and making sure that nothing falls through the cracks. It turns out that when we set out our intentions, we tend to keep them more often than not.

- Unscheduling is the radical opposite because it takes the focus off of work. In some ways, it is more realistic, because it dictates that you fill in your schedule with all of your nonnegotiables and life priorities. That way you can see how much time you actually have to work and think. It also allows you to see what is missing from your life and is harming you emotionally. Work comes last in this type of schedule, which is a weird thing to desire, but unless we have emotional energy and psychological comfort, then we will never get around to our tasks anyway, right?

- Paying more attention to your schedule and daily actions will result in some self-awareness and clarity about how you are spending your time. One thing to pay specific attention to is how much information you consume and at which point you are hitting the point of diminishing returns. As it turns out, much sooner than you might think, so you should consider going on an information diet and cutting out many of the sources of pure information in your life. They aren't doing you any good; they are probably mostly automatic behaviors that suck up your time and mental bandwidth.

Chapter 4. A Return to the Humble "To-Do" List

- A to-do list hastily written on a Post-It might be one of the most ubiquitous tools for self-discipline and avoiding procrastination. It works on our psychology by manipulating dopamine, and this is one of the few instances that we can actually make our brains work for us. But ultimately, a to-do list just makes sure that things are not being forgotten or falling through the cracks, and it doesn't necessarily assist you in doing more. It just prevents you from doing *less*. Thus, we need to level up the humble to-do list.

- We can start to do this by trimming the to-do list down to three items per day (yes, only three) to keep focused and lean. We can also set an intention or overall mission for the day and add only five (two big and three small) or nine (one big, three medium, and five small) tasks to the list in support of that mission. We can also add an element of reality-testing by evaluating your tasks through the metrics of seriousness, urgency, and growth in order to easily see what to prioritize.
- Another way to improve your to-do list is by using categories: immediate attention, in progress, follow-ups, upcoming, and ideas. This allows you to again sort by priority and make sure that you are properly addressing what needs to be addressed.
- The truth is that to-do lists often don't take context into account. Q1 and Q2

thinking solves that problem by forcing you to understand the difference between urgent and important. Most people don't have a grasp of these blurry lines, but it can mean all the difference in your output. Related to this is the don't-do list, also essentially seen in Q4 of the Eisenhower matrix. Most people know what they should be doing but not what they *shouldn't* be doing. This is where you eliminate tasks that (1) are insignificant, (2) are a poor use of your time, (3) don't help your bottom line or end purpose, and (4) have a serious case of diminishing returns the more you work on them.

Chapter 5. Adjust Your Psychology

- The final piece of the puzzle for greater self-discipline and sticking to your guns is to change your thoughts. Thoughts, of course, lead to behavior, and behavior is what we want to change in the end. In this chapter, we talk about three specific ways to change the way that you think about taking action versus lying on the couch.

- First, we come to the Ulysses pact, or as I would call it, coerced compliance. It's the act of burning your bridges and not allowing yourself to make a detrimental choice in the heat of the moment or out of a lack of self-awareness. When you find that you have no choice, and you must actually sit with your thoughts and work through things, that's just what you'll do. There is no easier path of least resistance, and there is no escape. If you can smartly plan and make this choice beforehand using commitment devices such as the Ulysses pact, then you no longer have to exercise self-discipline per se.

- Next, we come to the practice of discomfort and all that it entails. By definition, anything that requires exercising self-discipline is uncomfortable. We'd rather not do it, otherwise it would be known as fun. This puts us in a quandary; sometimes there is nothing else we can do but suck it up and push forward, despite all the tactics and mindsets we've discussed in this book. At some point, we will have to be uncomfortable, and sometimes life is just a matter of how much discomfort you can stomach. Thus, we must practice it, and we will eventually grow immune to an extent. Practicing discomfort is like a vaccine against your impulses and weak moments. When you can slowly gain perspective that discomfort is not so bad and ultimately temporary, you'll be amazed at what you can accomplish.

- Impulses are the polar opposite of self-discipline, and they are things we must consciously train against indulging in. Oh, but it's hard. Impulses are behind every subconscious thought that we struggle to rein in. How can we ever hope to combat this? Generally, we must try to interject space and time between a thought and an action. We can do this by simply counting slowly to 10, labeling your thoughts and feelings, writing down the facts of a situation, and asking yourself *why* five times and making sure to answer honestly.